Y0-CAS-612

Out of the Bleachers and onto the Field

How to Witness without Hang-ups

Michael E. Gibson

SAINT LOUIS

Unless otherwise stated, the Scripture quotations in this publication are from The Holy Bible: NEW INTERNATIONAL VERSION, © 1973, 1978, 1984 by the International Bible Society. Used by permission of Zondervan Bible Publishers.

Scripture quotations marked NET are taken from GOD'S WORD TO THE NATIONS: *New Testament—New Evangelical Translation.* Copyright © 1990 Mrs. William F. Beck. Used by permission of NET Publishing.

The quotations from the Lutheran Confessions in this publication are from *The Book of Concord: The Confessions of the Ev. Lutheran Church,* ed. by Theodore G. Tappert, Fortress Press © 1959. Used by permission of the publisher.

Copyright © 1992 Concordia Publishing House
3558 S. Jefferson Avenue, St. Louis, MO 63118-3968
Manufactured in the United States of America

All rights reserved. No part of this publication may be reproduced, stored in a retrieval system, or transmitted, in any form or by any means, electronic, mechanical, photocopying, recording, or otherwise, without the prior written permission of Concordia Publishing House.

1 2 3 4 5 6 7 8 9 10 VP 01 00 99 98 97 96 95 94 93 92

For Kathy, Andrew, and Tim.
The greatest team of all time.
You make my story a joy!

Contents

Foreword

"In order that this treasure might not be buried but put to use and enjoyed, God has caused the Word to be published and proclaimed." So Martin Luther wrote in his Large Catechism (II 38). The Gospel treasure is that God graciously declares us sinners righteous through Christ. Sadly, this wonderful Word is easily and often buried so that the Holy Spirit is not able to arouse faith.

One way the Gospel is "deep-sixed" is through religious jargon. "Words like *sin, justification, atonement, works, sanctification* have become shorthand ways of talking theology among professional church workers, but they are tough nuts to crack for the laity" (Prof. Mark Brighton, *Interconnections*, June 1992).

In OUT OF THE BLEACHERS AND ONTO THE FIELD Pastor Mike Gibson talks straight about using a loving and honest relationship with a non-Christian to present the true Christ of the Gospel, avoiding hallowed theological words. Indeed, at the proper time, when your friend has been enthralled by the wonderful Word and sets out to learn more of the Savior, and the scandal of the Crucified has been clearly presented, then bring out the theological words.

Clearly presented! When your friend decides to join a Christian congregation, the decision should be for the right reason. Conversely, rejecting the fellowship of God's people around Word and Sacraments should be for the right reason.

The reason to join or not to join is the scandal of the Crucified, that God became man in Christ, at the cross suffered the divine anger against sin, was raised, ascended, and now gathers his people by the Gospel, Baptism, and the Lord's Supper. Jesus Christ is "the very Stone—rejected by the builders—who has become the Cornerstone, a Stone which makes them stumble and a Rock which causes them to fall. Because they disobey the word, they stumble over it" (1 Peter 2:7–8 NET).

Witnessing is holy ground. Your genuine and loving relationship with a friend is a prelude to the Holy Spirit's miraculous working through the external and clear word of the Christ. "Through these [the Gospel and the Sacraments], as through means, [God] gives the Holy Spirit, who works faith, when and where He pleases, in those who hear the Gospel" (Augsburg Confession V). So read Pastor Gibson's good suggestions for getting out of the bleachers and onto the field with a constant prayer, "Come, Holy Spirit!"

Dr. Dale A. Meyer, *Speaker*
"The Lutheran Hour"

Introduction

"There's two balls and one strike now, Dad!"

I had just taught him how to read the scoreboard. That's about all there was to keep a five-year-old interested. It was one of those games where the pitchers reigned and the batters struck out. The San Francisco Giants were playing the Pittsburgh Pirates in a night game at Candlestick Park.

"A night game at the 'Stick!' " That one phrase is enough to make any Giants' fan shiver. Andrew and I had on our coats, gloves, stocking caps, and a blanket. He was sitting on my lap, not only because that's a fun thing to do, but because two bodies together stay warmer than one alone.

Welcome to San Francisco in August! Mark Twain was right, you know: "The coldest winter I ever spent was one summer in San Francisco."

I had given up trying to point out the fine points of a ball game dominated by pitching. Andrew had learned to read the scoreboard, that was enough for him.

"Dad, I'm going to watch the game by looking at the scoreboard."

The pitcher threw the ball toward home plate.

"Three balls and two strikes," he roared.

His call came through loud and clear. It wasn't meant for me alone. He was sitting on my lap, I could hear him just fine.

The report from this self-proclaimed chairman of the "board" was for the benefit of everyone within hearing distance, just in case they hadn't learned to read the scoreboard for themselves.

Andrew didn't care what was happening down on the field, where the teams attempted to play in the cold, whipping wind. He liked his perspective. He was warm and safe on my lap. He knew the count and the score; that was all that mattered.

It's amazing how much a person can learn about life and faith from the attitude of this particular five-year-old. I'm really not all that different from him. I would like having my own perspective too, being able to look down on life from a safe, warm distance, seated in the eternal lap of my heavenly Father and knowing the score.

When it comes to faith, we Christians feel pretty safe. As a result, we have a tendency to think only about our circumstances and forget that others around us have not experienced the love and warmth of salvation in Jesus Christ. The challenge before us Christians, when it comes to the issue of faith, is to get out of the bleachers and live out our faith on the field of life. We are to take it with us wherever we go, to every situation and relationship that comes our way. The Lord never intended for us to sit back, satisfied and grateful to have faith, and watch those who do not know him as Savior and Lord struggle through life without God and without hope. "Climb down from the bleachers," he insists, "and involve yourselves in the lives of others so that they might come to know him too."

Their stories are wide and varied. Some grew up in church and Sunday school but later walked away from the Lord. Their reasons are many, and all of them are unsatisfying. Others don't even have a clue! They have never heard, or just have not paid attention to, the message of a Savior who loves them and offers a new life in exchange for their old one. Many are looking for life's answers in a variety of different places, wrapping up in any available blanket, but finding no warmth.

Others are trying out all the empty laps in sight, but never finding real safety, or they are looking at every scoreboard that is lit, but finding only zeros. We know many of them personally. Some of them are named: Dad and Mom, Uncle John, Cousin Fred, Joanne (with whom we have lunch at work), Paul (that cute boy in the second row of biology class). Many carry titles such as husband, wife, son, and daughter.

Their circumstances need to matter to us. Most of us who know the score and are safe in the arms of our heavenly Father do care about our unbelieving family and friends. But we have hesitated to get out of the bleachers so that the

Lord can use us to help change their lives. What keeps us off the field? Lots of things! Most of them have to do with fear and just not knowing where to start or what to say.

This book offers *cross* training in hopes of answering some of those concerns, removing some of the hang-ups and guilt we feel, and opening up a whole new world of discovering what it means to share our faith with others.

"We win!"

The announcement came in the midst of a yawn from a warm, cozy, sleepy, little boy. It was getting pretty late.

"We can stand up now, Daddy, it's time to get going."

We do win when we trust in Jesus as our Savior. But for many others, it is getting pretty late. It is time for us to get going, before it gets any later—out of the bleachers and onto the field.

Chapter 1

Welcome to the Team!

He just wouldn't look up!

Justice had his eyes glued to the documents in front of him. It was hard to fault his concentration. He wasn't the usual judge for this kind of case. He was just filling in. He had to make sure everything was correct; it was his job.

No matter how many times the 17-month-old on my lap looked across the desk and spoke, the judge just wouldn't look up.

"Hi!"

Still no response!

Undaunted, the little voice came forth again, this time with extra volume, the vowel held long for emphasis, his limited vocabulary filling the judge's chambers.

"Hiieee!!"

The eyes of justice began to move, finally acknowledging the interruption and softening into a smile. The subject matter of our hearing that day was finally acknowledged: one rambunctious bundle of blond-haired energy who was about to be sentenced to life as a Gibson.

That's when the important stuff began:

"Mike and Kathy, as Andrew's adoptive parents, will you commit to provide all that he needs in life: clothing, food, housing, and education?"

"Yes," we answered. (Hey, this was going to be easy!)

"Will you welcome him into your family and incorporate him into the extended family of grandparents, cousins, aunts, uncles, and the like?"

"Yes!" (Little did he know how many people at church had already claimed this rambunctious bundle as theirs. This kid would never want for extended family!)

"Will you absolutely guarantee Andrew his inheritance? Now, before you answer, let me explain that biological parents can disinherit their children, adoptive parents cannot."

Now, of course our answer was going to be "Yes," but it sure brought to mind a few unvoiced thoughts and questions. This was a whole new issue.

What if Andrew turns out to be a real creep and doesn't deserve an inheritance? His inheritance would be guaranteed.

If he says, "Mom and Dad, keep the inheritance, I don't want it!" we've still got to offer it. We've got to keep our promise!

What if he runs off, changes his mind, comes back and asks for his inheritance? Guaranteed!

The voice of justice brought me back to the hearing. "Mike and Kathy, will you guarantee Andrew his inheritance?"

"Absolutely!" we responded in unison.

After a few appropriately placed signatures and the stamp of the Seal of the Great State of California, Andrew Michael Gibson was adopted. He was still the same 17-month-old baby. He looked the same, talked the same, slept in the same crib, ate just as sloppily as he always did, and was loved by those who had always loved him, only now he had been given something that could never be taken away from him. This same little boy had a new name, a new life, parents committed to his care, and a guaranteed inheritance. A chapter in the Gibson family was all his own. Through the act of adoption, the story of all of those who lived before him and carried the name Gibson was now his!

The judge didn't know it, but I wanted to give him a hug!

He had just preached one of the greatest sermons I'd ever heard, explaining what happens when we become part of God's eternal family through Baptism: We receive a new name, a new identity, the guarantee of a glorious inheritance, and a rich heritage and history as part of the family of God. We never stop being part of that team as long as we keep our faith in Christ. The great thing is that the Lord is not sitting up in the bleachers. He is Emmanuel! God is with us, right on the field of our lives as we live day to day.

I have the privilege of pastoring an exciting congregation in the south San Francisco Bay area: Mount Olive Lutheran Church in Milpitas. At

Mount Olive we are into babies: infant babies, teenage babies, 60-year-old babies, every kind of baby! We love to see people come to know Jesus and become newly born children of God, and through Baptism we have the joy of welcoming them to the team!

Their whole history changes. The story of God working in the lives of his people since the beginning of time now becomes theirs. In our baptismal service we even say, "Jesus' story becomes your story." That story includes a new chapter every day as the Lord involves himself in the lives of his people. That is the reason that our stories are unique and provide us with the substance of what we can share with others.

Witnessing Is Storytelling

The room was full of pastors from many different places and denominations. Some of them were very well known in the Christian world and pastored large churches, others were known only to the people who make up their congregations. All of us were asked to spend five minutes telling the others about ourselves, telling our story. The problem with that kind of an assignment is not what to say, but what to leave out. If I had been asked to introduce one of the other class members, filling five minutes would be tough. It would lack the personal touch and wouldn't give a clear picture of the individual. But since I was to talk about myself, I knew I could handle that. I know me better than anyone else!

It's the same kind of thing when it comes to sharing our faith with others. God hasn't called us to talk about something we know nothing about. He has called us to tell our story. That story includes the Lord's involvement in the ups and downs, the failures and successes in our lives. We get to talk about how Jesus brings his forgiveness to the times when we blow it. We get to talk about how our all-providing God has brought more blessings into our lives than we could ever recall.

We are always telling our story, whether we are consciously aware of it or not. Through faith, God has made us part of his team. We never stop being part of that team; that's the exciting thing about a guaranteed inheritance. Everything we do and everything we say sets our life story before others, and don't think for a minute that your unchurched friends and family members aren't watching; they are!

What an awesome story it is: You and I interacting with the God of all creation. It is a story of his faithfulness in the midst of our faithlessness, nothing more, nothing less!

The early Christians understood this type of witnessing. It is easily seen in Acts 4, where Peter and John were speaking to the people about Jesus, telling of his resurrection from the dead. Many people came to faith because of their message, but not everyone was happy about it. The church leaders had Peter and John arrested and brought before their supreme religious court for a hearing. This court, the Sanhedrin, could be a rather imposing bunch. They didn't mince words. They made it very clear to the disciples that they were not to "speak or teach at all in the name of Jesus" (Acts 4:18).

Now, you and I might have heard the warning and decided to just drop the whole thing, but not Peter and John. They had an interesting response. Look at verses 19 and 20.

> But Peter and John replied, "Judge for yourselves whether it is right in God's sight to obey you rather than God. For we cannot help speaking about what we have seen and heard."

Did you see it? Did you see their method of witnessing in their words to the Sanhedrin? Look at it again:

"We cannot help speaking about what we have seen and heard."

The message that they were speaking in the temple courts every day was not something with which they were unfamiliar. They were talking about THEIR experience with the crucified and risen Savior, Jesus Christ. They spoke about what THEY had seen and heard.

Their story brought to the message the critical ingredient of their personal touch. When John and Peter told the people of God's love for them in Jesus, they were able to point to their own lives, affected and changed, as living examples.

Peter and John were able to bring a passion to what they had to say because it was important to them, it was THEIR story, THEIR encounter with Jesus.

The Apostle Paul: A Master Storyteller

The apostle Paul was the greatest evangelist of the Scriptures. He was very effective in what he did, evidenced by the many people who came to faith through his ministry. How did Paul do it? He told his story! Let me show you an example.

Toward the end of Paul's recorded ministry in the book of Acts, we read about his final return to Jerusalem. The reception he received was not what you would call a warm one. A riot erupted and Paul was arrested! At one point the crowd became so incensed that the soldiers had to carry Paul for fear that the people would kill him.

I would have been running out of town as fast as my legs could carry me. You probably would too! Paul, of course, was another story.

"Please let me speak to the people" (Acts 21:39).

Now, you might think that Paul would argue that he was not doing anything wrong. After all, he had simply come to the temple area for seven days of ritual purification.

Wrong! Look at chapter 22, beginning with verse 3.

I am a Jew, born in Tarsus of Cilicia, but brought up in this city. Under Gamaliel I was thoroughly trained in the law of our fathers and was just as zealous for God as any of you are today.

What is he doing? He is not defending himself at all. If you read on you will discover that he is telling his story!

He tells about persecuting the Christians, about his blinding conversion on the road to Damascus, and, when he regained his sight, how Ananias explained the message of Jesus to him. Paul is telling his story of the Lord's involvement in his life, nothing more, nothing less.

Paul remained in jail for two years. During that time, he had hearings before governors Felix and Festus and eventually King Agrippa. Now, you might expect that Paul would have spent the better part of that two-year period in the prison's law library, carefully preparing his case so that he would be ready to quote chapter and verse of previous decisions that would work in his favor. But, then again, you've probably figured out that Paul seldom does what we think he'll do! Paul tells his story, again! Check out chapter 26.

Why does he tell his story again and again? It is what he knows best. His story provides a contemporary context for the story of Jesus' work of salvation. Paul is a living, breathing example to which his hearers can relate.

Your story is no different!

Each Story Is Important

I made a new friend not too long ago. Talk about a story! He is the pastor of a big church in

Southern California. But he hasn't always walked closely with the Lord. His story is one that goes from the depths of sin to the pinnacle of God's forgiveness and glory. It is dramatic, it is exciting, and it is wonderful. God has greatly used his story to affect the lives of many people. God wants to use your story too!

I can hear what you're thinking: "But I don't have a story like that. My story is boring when you compare it to someone with a dramatic conversion experience. No one is interested in hearing what I have to say!"

That's where you are wrong!

Dramatic accounts of God's saving power in the lives of people are exciting and entertaining to hear, but most people do not come to know the Lord Jesus that way. Most of us come to Jesus in very gentle ways.

Many of us were brought to the waters of Baptism by loving parents when we were little babies. There are few things more gentle and wonderful than that. That's when the Lord made us part of his team and guaranteed his involvement in our lives today and the certainty of our inheritance in eternity. There was just as big a party in heaven the day you entered the Kingdom through Baptism as there is when God saves someone in an incredibly dramatic way.

Some of us were brought to faith when a person who cared about us shared the message of Jesus.

When we heard about his love, his death, and his resurrection, God's Spirit sparked faith in us, and enabled us to know Jesus as Savior and Lord. Fireworks probably didn't go off where you were, but heaven certainly erupted in celebration.

I have had the opportunity to be present with many people as the Lord brought them into a saving relationship with him. Those occasions usually occurred in someone's living room, while on a walk, or while having a cup of coffee. Were those conversions any less dramatic than others? Absolutely not! There is no way that the effect of conversion could ever be minimized in the life of an individual; it is the single greatest event in someone's life.

Your story is important! The Lord wants you to share your story of his involvement in your life with others who are just like you. You see, they will be able to relate to your story best. Your life provides the Gospel with a context that they understand. Because they know you and trust you, they will be willing to hear and see what you have to say and do.

If we wait for those who have incredible stories of conversion to share their faith with those we know and love, we might wait a long time. God hasn't called them to share their faith with your neighbor, spouse, classmate, or fellow worker. He has called you! That's why you have a relationship with them. The Lord has provided a customized channel through which his story can be shared: YOU! That's how God has grown his church throughout the centuries; one person touching the life of another with his or her story of Jesus.

I came to know Jesus as my Savior and Lord in December 1956 when I was baptized as a infant. There is never a time in my life when I didn't know Jesus to be my Savior. Oh, there were rough times along the way. I did a pretty good job trying to run away from him. But every time I turned around, there stood my heavenly Father with his arms outstretched, welcoming me back and affirming that my inheritance was still intact. You see, my story is a great example of God's perfect faithfulness in the midst of my inconsistency. It is God taking me just as I am but not letting me stay that way.

I think that my simple story, with its details that make it particularly mine, of the Lord's faithfulness in the life of a normal, everyday sinner is powerful. Why? Because most of the people I know are in the same boat. They can relate to a story like mine.

They can understand a story like yours.

So, what's your story?

Onto the Field

At the end of each chapter you will have the opportunity to apply what you have read to your own experience. Please accept the challenge to get out of the bleachers and onto the field by working through each of the exercises. You may want to turn a notebook into your own personalized witnessing book.

1. When did your adoption (Baptism) take place? Where were you baptized? Who was the pastor? Who was on your baptismal team (parents, sponsors/godparents)? Write the date of your baptismal rebirth on the calendar and commit to celebrating that day just as you do the day of your physical birth.

2. Read the story of the prodigal son, Luke 15:11–32. Take some time to think about your personal story as it relates to the parable. Does your story reflect the experience of the prodigal son, the father, or the elder brother? How have you treated the wonderful inheritance that you have been guaranteed by your heavenly Father?

3. Jim and Allison have been married for about a year. When they met, Jim knew that she attended church. Since their wedding day, Allison has been encouraging Jim to go with her. He's hesitant, he's never been to church except for a wedding or a funeral. One day during a coffee break at work he asks you, "My wife keeps inviting me to go to church with her. I'd do anything for her, but I'm just not sure about this church stuff. I know that you go to a church, too. Why do you go? What does it do for you?" What would you say to Jim? What part of your story about Jesus' involvement in your life would you share with him that will answer his question? You may find it helpful to write your answer.

Chapter 2

Getting Ready

Only 89 days until the first game of spring training!

I have a confession to make. I am a Baseball Junkie. I don't imagine that there are too many people who count down the days remaining until the first game of the new season. I can't help it. It must be in my blood. My wife thinks it's all in my head!

The crack of the bat, the smell of freshly mown grass and hot dogs, the crunch of peanut shells under your feet, freezing to death at Candlestick Park. (Wait a minute, that one's not supposed to be in there.) I don't want to miss a minute of the season. When the umpire yells, "Play ball," I want to be prepared!

When you think about it, my little ritual of preparation is nothing compared to what the teams are doing to get ready. Throughout the offseason there are trades to be made, minor leaguers to sign, and salaries to be arbitrated. The players are not waiting until the first day of spring training to get into shape; they are working to maintain their critical physical conditioning.

When training camp does begin, there are new faces to meet and a lot of work to be done. A lot takes place before play ever begins on the field. The players and the front-office people are intentional about their task, because a great deal is at stake.

Most of my passion for baseball is limited to what I do as a spectator. That is not the case when it comes to being part of God's team, the church. Through the faith that God has given me through Christ, I have a guaranteed contract with a no-trade clause! I am a child of God through Jesus Christ. His work of salvation makes me an active participant, not a spectator. Sitting in the bleachers is not an option. No "Pew Potato" here! The action takes place where I live, on the field of life.

I am not alone on the field. Some are part of God's team, others are not. But the Lord has brought his team together so that others might find out what is offered to them in Jesus Christ and enter into his glorious inheritance. There is certainly a lot at stake.

Effective Witnessing Takes Preparation

I had always thought that witnessing began when I opened my mouth and started talking (most preachers feel that way about a lot of things), but that's not the case at all. I've discovered that while my words are an important ingredient in witnessing, what the Lord is doing behind the scenes is absolutely critical. He is doing a work of preparation that should not be overlooked. Nothing is ever going to happen in witnessing unless the "front office" lays the foundation. It clears the way for the witnessing that will be played out later on the field of life. The Lord prepares for every witnessing event in two ways. First, he is at work preparing you and me to witness, while, at the same time, he is getting the person ready with whom we are going to speak.

Those already on his team he takes through an exercise that we could call evangelistic spring training. First, through his Word he covers the basics, reminding us of our salvation; pointing us to the task of making disciples; and promising that he will not only be with us when we speak of Jesus but that he will also provide the words to say. Additionally, he allows us to have experiences in life that add to our story, providing a contemporary context for the Gospel, that will make sharing easier.

At the same time, in a variety of ways he prepares people who are apart from him to hear our witness about Jesus and his involvement in our life story. Others, people we don't even know, are praying for them to be saved. Still others are speaking words of Gospel to them even before we speak (remember, you may not be the only person witnessing to this individual), and the Lord is allowing experiences to occur in their own lives that show them their need for him.

Let me take you to the Old Testament, to the story of Joseph, to show you an example of just how much God cares about preparing people for the work he is planning to do.

Joseph: An Example of God's Preparation

Not many families could boast enough boys to field their own football team. Jacob's family sure could; there were 12 of them. (Can you imagine the food bill?) One would expect a little sibling rivalry in any family of this size, and this clan was no exception. The brothers knew exactly whom to pick on: Joseph, Dad's favorite. He would do just fine.

It's helpful to go to the end of the story to see the Lord's plan and how the careful step-by-step preparation comes together. God knew that there was to be a famine and that this family of 12 children was probably going to be in need of some AFDC (Aid for Families with Dependent Children). He wanted the people of Israel to become a nation, large in number. For that to occur, they needed food, work, and a peaceful existence. Somehow he had to get them all to Egypt. Now, watch the progression as God's plan of preparation goes into action.

Joseph is thrown into a pit by his brothers and eventually sold into slavery. Remarkably, he ends up as the manager of the household of Pharaoh's captain of the guard, a guy named Potiphar. That, however, wasn't high enough up the political ladder to insure the relocation of Joseph's father and family and the growth of Israel. Something else needed to happen.

Potiphar's wife steps in to move the process forward. Mrs. Potiphar was not what you would call a "good girl." Her roving eye had her following Joseph around the house, trying to convince him to become the "other man," to have an affair with her. Jacob's son responds to this invitation in the manner in which we hope all of our children will, he declines. Now Mrs. Potiphar is used to getting her way and will not take no for an answer. A struggle ensues and Joseph runs out of the house, minus his clothes. What do you do if you're Mrs. Potiphar and someone sees a naked man running out of your house? You scream, "Rape!"

It doesn't take much of a rocket scientist to realize that Joseph will come out on the losing end when Captain Potiphar returns home. Joseph ends up in the dungeon of the city jail (sure seems like he has a thing for the pits) where he develops a new job description, Interpreter of Dreams.

It just so happens that Pharaoh was having a little trouble sleeping, something about fat and skinny cows and heads of grain. The cupbearer of Pharaoh, who had earlier benefited from Joseph's dream interpretation, recommends that Pharaoh consult Joseph.

The rest, as they say, is history. From his position as dungeon steward and part-time dream interpreter, Joseph is promoted to the top floor of the capitol building, to a corner office with a view, a corporate American Express card, and a key to the executive washroom. What happens from there? Reconciliation with his brothers, a reunion with his father, and the whole family's permanent move to Egypt, to an environment where the Lord could build them into a great nation.

Was that all a nice coincidence? If it was, it probably came out of Hollywood. God was at work! He was hard at work in Joseph, in Pharaoh, and in all the other cast members to accomplish his purposes for his people.

Here's where we come in: will the Lord do that for us today? Will he put that kind of effort into preparing an environment for our witnessing? Absolutely!

Our God wants all people to be saved and to come to the knowledge of the truth. That's right out of 1 Tim. 2:4. And, since it's God's Word, we can believe it! Now, here's an action point: while the Lord will do everything necessary to prepare the hearer and the speaker for the communication of the Gospel, someone still has to speak the words. Want some Scripture support for this? Try Rom. 10:14.

> "How, then, can they call on the one they have not believed in? And how can they believe in the one of whom they have not heard? And how can they hear without someone preaching to them?"

That is a rather pragmatic verse. It carries with it an intentional attitude toward the unsaved, the same attitude that we need to develop ourselves.

Effective Witnessing Is Intentional

I had one of those crazy kind of friends in college. Let's call him Joe—that's not his real name, but this guy needs all the anonymity he can get! He would try anything once. If he lived through it, he'd probably do it again. As crazy as he was, he had an even crazier car. It was a little VW Bug that looked like he had purchased it off the demolition derby lot. He drove it just the way he lived the rest of his life: full speed ahead. The interesting thing about the car was that the passenger seat was not bolted to the floor. Riding with Joe was like sitting in a rocking chair with wheels. I never fully understood why Volkswagen put hand straps in their cars until I rode with Joe.

Every once in a while I'd let him drive me to class. We had a routine we followed. Joe would open up the passenger's door (his door was jammed shut from an accident), shove my seat back and climb into his. I'd get in, pick up the seat to adjust it for my height (I'm 6'4''), shut the door and hang on for dear life.

It really got interesting when it rained. We followed the same format with one exception. The car had no windshield wipers. Once situated, I would roll the window down while Joe reached behind his seat to hand me a plastic bag with the bottom cut out of it. I would slide it over my right arm and secure it with rubber bands at my wrist and elbow. Next, he would hand me a long-handled squeegee, which I would push and pull across the windshield. And, without so much as a moment's hesitation, Joe would take off down the street, never quite sure where we were or where we were going!

Out of all that silliness emerges a true description of the way an awful lot of people go about witnessing. They have no idea where to begin, where they are, or where they are going. Allow me to point us in the right direction. Intentionally build relationships with unchurched people. Whether we are talking about living or witnessing, it works best to have a plan. Step 1 of any workable witnessing plan is this: develop friendships with some non-Christians. When we do that, the Lord will do the preparation work to provide the experiences that open the door for sharing our faith.

Target a Relationship

If we are going to do some witnessing, it's sure helpful to know to whom we are going to witness. Have someone in mind? Family member, that guy at work, that cute cheerleader you keep thinking about asking out on a date, neighbor, son or daughter? (This list could go on forever!) Allow me to share with you my process. It may or may not work for you. That's fine, but what it might do is to get your creative juices flowing.

Prayer

The most important part of my day is the time I spend before the Lord in prayer. During my prayer time I regularly ask the Lord to bring to mind the names of individuals with whom I might share the message of Jesus. As I think of names, I write them on a list that I keep in my prayer journal. Next, I pray for them. I pray for opportunities to share my faith. I pray for boldness to open my mouth when the opportunities come.

Limitations

I know my limitations. I know that if I really tried to share my faith in a substantial way with everyone on my list, I would do a poor job. I have learned to concentrate on just a few at a time. (I don't forget about the others. Remember, I'm praying for them regularly and, if opportunities come, I open my mouth and share.) I know that if I invest my efforts in just one or two people at a time in a very intentional manner, the Lord is going to be able to use me much more effectively in the work that he is doing.

Create a Friendship

I have also discovered that people are much more interested in what I have to say about my faith if my sharing happens within the context of a friendship. I have a friend whom I really enjoy. He is on my list. I have spent a good deal of time pursuing the growth of our friendship. When I see him I do not just wave to him, I go over and chat. When things happen to me and my family, I make sure I share those with him. He's doing the same with me now. He's been over for dinner, enjoyed some time soaking in our spa, and even helped me paint the house.

Here is an important thing to remember: This is not a contrived friendship. I am not building a relationship just so I can share Jesus with him. He is my friend. I like him. I want to spend time with him and have him in my home. And, since I enjoy being with him, I also want him to be with me in heaven.

Is the Lord doing his work of preparation in our relationship? You bet he is! When God's team is moving on the field of life, the front office is doing incredible things for the advancement of the Gospel. It's great to know that the Lord has a plan for my friend and for our relationship. I'm excited that I get to be part of it.

Onto the Field

1. God is about the work of using our life experiences to prepare us for the opportunity of telling our faith story. Think back over the last week; what have you experienced that can be identified as a new chapter in your faith story? How can God use that new chapter to communicate the Gospel to someone else?

2. Write down the names of your unsaved friends and family members. Who on that list is a person with whom you would like to share your faith? Remember, the Lord is right now preparing you to share, and your friend to hear, the story of your life with Jesus. Commit yourself to pray for God to do his powerful work of preparation in you and in the person you have targeted for opportunities to witness. If you keep a written record, later you'll have the joy of seeing the Lord of Work at work, possibly in surprising ways.

Chapter 3

Making Contact

One of these days I'm going to catch one!

I am aggressively instilling the desire in Andrew, and as soon as Timmy is old enough to understand, he's next. Lots of people at ball games catch foul balls (not that I've ever caught one). I want to catch a home run. You know, the kind of hit that has a crowd rising to its feet and roaring the moment it leaves the bat, following its flight path into the outfield stands.

We always sit in the right-field stands; it is called the Family Pavilion. It's a great place for kids: no drinking, no smoking, no foul language allowed. It is also a great place for grown men to chase home runs! (Isn't it amazing how a silly game can bring out the child in the man?)

While the home-run hitter is exciting and helps to fill the stands, it is the contact hitter who consistently wins games night after night. He's not going to have the big home-run numbers, but he will have a nice batting average. When he's up at the plate, he's just looking to make contact, to put the ball in play. He's the one who gets on base more times than not and drives in runs.

When it comes to witnessing, the Lord has not called us to hit a home run every time, but he does want us to make contact. It is certainly wonderful when someone comes to faith in Christ as a result of your witnessing. That obviously is the goal, but it is not going to happen every time. Putting the Gospel of Jesus into play on the field of life is what it is all about. God will bring the home runs of conversion when we focus on making contact.

Using Cross Points to Make Contact

In the previous chapter, we discussed how the Lord is in the process of preparing both speaker and hearer for witnessing, for making contact. Each person is learning and experiencing things in life that God will use to communicate the Gospel. From time to time, both our life experiences will cross; they will overlap. I call these moments of overlap "Cross Points." Our life's story provides the contemporary context for the message of the Cross. As our life's story makes contact with someone else's, God puts the Gospel into play.

Let me give you an example of what I'm talking about. Several years ago while participating in an evangelism training clinic in Houston, I had the opportunity to call on a man whom we will call Roger. He had recently attended church at the congregation hosting the clinic. It was the job of the visitation team to call on Roger and, if possible, to share the Gospel. During our conversation, I discovered that Roger was having a tough time understanding what it meant that salvation through Jesus Christ was a free gift from God, something that we cannot pay for or even deserve. Few things in life are free, and Roger was well aware of it.

We had already discovered that Roger was a big sports fan. (There was a cast on his leg as a result of a hard slide into second base.) Knowing this, the Lord brought to mind a story from my own life that provided a real-life context for Roger to understand the Gospel.

I had recently attended a baseball game with a group from my congregation. As usually happens, we had a couple of no-shows and were stuck with two tickets. I started walking through the crowd waiting in line to buy tickets. I didn't want to sell the tickets, just give them away. Everyone I approached looked at me as if I was crazy. "What's the catch? You don't want anything for them?" Actually, the whole process was driving me crazy. The game was ready to start, and I wanted to get into the stadium with my friends. Finally I cornered (and I mean cornered) two teenage boys and managed to convince them that the tickets were absolutely free, no strings attached! They took them, and I finally got to see the game.

As I finished my story, Roger's eyes lit up: "That happened to me last week at a Houston Rockets basketball game. A guy came up to me and gave me a free ticket. It was the best seat I've ever had. Now I understand what you're talking about when you say salvation is a free gift from God."

What happened between Roger and me? The Lord made contact by providing a Cross Point! Little did Roger or I know that when we had those experiences the Lord was going to use them to provide a context for his message of salvation that was common to us both.

An Altar to an Unknown God: Paul's Cross Point

The ministry of the apostle Paul recorded in Acts 17 provides a great example of the use of Cross Points in communicating the Gospel. Paul was the new kid in town; he hadn't been in Athens very long. Since arriving, he'd spent his time walking around town, looking and listening to the city and its people. Every day he spoke in the synagogue and marketplace, succeeding in attracting the attention of some of the local intellectuals. As a result, Paul was asked to speak at the Areopagus, where the real brains of the day hung out; all sorts of philosophy and new ways of thinking were debated. (Notice how he starts his message in verses 22 and 23.)

> Paul then stood up in the meeting of the Areopagus and said: "Men of Athens! I see that in every way you are very religious. For as I walked around and looked carefully at your objects of worship, I even found an altar with this inscription: TO AN UNKNOWN

GOD. Now what you worship as something unknown I am going to proclaim to you."

What happened at the Areopagus? Paul's words made contact. God enabled what was known both to Paul and to those gathered at the Areopagus to become an opportunity for the Gospel. He used a Cross Point, a reality in their lives that provided a contemporary context to express the truth of Jesus Christ. Was Paul effective? Did the Lord use Paul's words and choice of a Cross Point to bring people to faith? Look at verse 34. "A few men became followers of Paul and believed."

We have seen two examples of Paul's method of sharing the Gospel of Jesus Christ with others: at the Areopagus and previously before King Agrippa. Both include excellent descriptions of God's love in Jesus; one, however, was more effective.

When Paul stood before Agrippa, he gave a moving account of the story of God's involvement in his life. While Agrippa was interested in what Paul had to say, he did not express faith in the Lord Jesus. Why not? If you look at that passage again in Acts 26, you will discover that there was something missing: a Cross Point that spoke to Agrippa's life. Let me show you what I mean.

When Paul spoke to Agrippa, he did so as one Jew to another, communicating a shared sense of history and heritage. Agrippa, as a puppet king of Rome, was greatly influenced by

Rome's culture and ways. Paul's message focused on their common Jewish heritage but lacked a contemporary Cross Point that enabled the Gospel to speak to Agrippa's current life situation. Why didn't Agrippa come to faith in Christ? The answer is really quite simple. Because Paul was in prison, he did not have an opportunity to get to know Agrippa before he told his story; he was merely summoned to appear. In Athens, on the other hand, Paul had the chance to get to know the people a little.

Remember, before Paul ever appeared at the Areopagus, he walked through the city and spoke in the synagogue and in the marketplace "day by day" (that means more than just once or twice). Because he got a feel for the city and his audience, he was able to apply the Gospel to their lives. That's the reason the Lord was able to use Paul's witness in Athens to bring people to saving faith. Is there a lesson for our witnessing here? You bet there is!

Listen for Cross Points

I am about to share with you the most important tool in effective witnessing. It is what we learn from Paul's experiences. Are you ready? You've got to pay attention, it's only one word. LISTEN!

Disappointed? You shouldn't be!

Listening is the critical ingredient in sharing your story with someone else. Now before you get confused, let me affirm that you do need to open your mouth in order to witness. What I'm trying to impress upon you here is that you have to listen first so that you know WHAT to share and HOW to share it.

When I speak with those who are on my "witness list," I am always listening for openings for the Gospel where my life and theirs touch, for Cross Points. As our relationship grows, so do the number and depth of the Cross Points. Let me provide a personal example of the kind of growth that I'm talking about.

Three blocks from our house is a shopping center with a nice little grocery store. It is not the store where we do our "big shopping," but it is the place where we run whenever we need a couple of items or are in a hurry. (With a six-year-old and an infant in the house, that's just about all the time!) Because I usually buy only a few items at a time, I get to stand in the "10 Items or Less" line. It's supposed to be faster, but I think it's an advertising ploy for ignorant husbands. (It always irritates me that the guy ahead of me can't count. I know he's just like me, another ignorant husband on a shopping mission for his wife, but if I can see he's got 12 things in his basket, why can't he?) The same clerk always seems to be running the register. I've been in there enough that she recognizes me now; it hasn't always been like that. A little green dot changed things.

I wear a little colored dot on my wrist watch. I change the color to suit my mood, but its purpose always stays the same. Every time I look at my watch, the dot asks me one question: Have I spent time with the Lord today in Bible study and prayer? (Hey, don't laugh, it works for me!)

One day the clerk asked if I was a pilot. (That one confused me.)

"Pardon me?"

"The little green dot on your watch; are you a pilot?"

"No." (My expression must have given away my confusion.)

"My brother is training to be a pilot, and he has a dot on his watch; it has something or other to do with his pilot training."

(I was happy to know that she didn't know what she was talking about either.)

"If you're not a pilot, why do you wear a little green dot on your watch?"

(BINGO!)

I went on to tell her its purpose for me.

"Oh!" she replied. "Your total is $7.32."

(I think my explanation confused her.)

A couple of days later I was back in line. My dot was red this time.

"You've changed the color of your dot."

"Yep. If I don't, it loses its impact."

"Did it work today, did you remember?"

"Remember?"

"Your time with, you know, . . . God."

"Yeah, I did; I had a great time."

"Oh. Your total is $3.21."

(All I needed was ice cream this time.)

What was happening? My dot had become our Cross Point! Sure, I know it sounds dumb, but I'll never stand in her line without one. Since that time, our relationship and the number of Cross Points have grown. We have progressed to sharing pictures of children, the fact that I am a pastor, the death of her mother (mine died a few years ago, too), and a concern over a possible job layoff at the store. As we have our little talks (remember, I'm in the quick-check line), I try to remember previous conversations so that I can ask questions about her well-being in hopes of providing an opportunity to encourage her, to promise to pray for her, to speak to her about the Lord. I'm not doing anything special, just trying to make contact. And as I listen to her, I begin to get a feel for who she is and how she might respond to parts of my story.

Take the Time to Remember

When people are willing to speak about their personal life, it is common courtesy to pay attention. Don't let it go in one ear and out the other. If there is ever a time when you want to remember things about your conversations, it is during witnessing.

I keep a sheet in my journal for each of the individuals I am praying for (we'll talk more about this later). It's not a big job; remember, I know my limitations and am only focusing on a few people at a time. I jot down things that I remember about our last conversation and ideas for future witnessing opportunities. In other words, I write down their story, recognizing that the Lord has been using those experiences to prepare them for the witnessing I will do. As I pray for them, I will frequently review the list and ask God to bring to mind things in my story that will provide a Cross Point and a real-life context for the Gospel to be shared in their lives.

Cross Points can be almost anything, i.e., the birth of a baby, a new job, an *A* on a test, a discouraging visit to the doctor, the new movie that you both have seen, even a silly green dot. The thing that matters most is that it is a shared experience, something to which you can both relate and through which the Gospel can, in some way, be shared. You're the expert on your Cross Points. Take the time to identify how you can make contact with that person on your list and then watch how God works. It will surprise you!

Onto the Field

At the end of chapter 2, you had the opportunity to make a list of unsaved friends and family members. On this page, or in your notebook, write the names of one, two, or three individuals upon whom you have chosen to focus your witnessing efforts. List some Cross Points that you have in common with each person and begin to consider how they can be used by the Lord as contemporary contexts for the Gospel message you will share. Be sure to include these people in your prayers.

Chapter 4

Practice the Basics

Vince Lombardi. Now there's a name for you! When you think of football in the decade of the 1960s, the Green Bay Packers, coached by the great Vince Lombardi, have got to be near the top of your list. In our day and age, when professional football coaches seem to come and go as quickly as the weather, Lombardi's dynasty at Green Bay seems pretty impressive. As a result of his tenure and accomplishments, there are more than a few stories that have formed the mythology surrounding Vince Lombardi. One such story fits our purposes.

One Sunday the Packers played terribly; they were beaten at almost every aspect of the game. During the team meeting on the first day of practice following the game, Lombardi had a few words to share with his team. As he stood before them, football in hand, face stoic in determination, he said, "Today we go back to the basics. Gentlemen, this is a football!"

Frequently in the sports world, mistakes are made during games because care was not given to the basics, the fundamentals. Likewise, when teams are successful, they are said to be "fundamentally sound." The same is true when it comes to witnessing. Knowing the basics is critical.

I am convinced that the most effective witnessing occurs in relationships where one person tells another a personal story of life with Jesus Christ. That kind of conversation happens naturally and is never contrived, but there is a dynamic that occurs of which we must be aware.

As our relationships deepen, the conversations regarding our faith should deepen as well. More and more Cross Points will be discovered, which will provide additional opportunities to discuss who Jesus is, why he had to die, what the resurrection means, and more. The Lord tells us in 1 Peter 3:15 that we need to be able to discuss these important topics; we need to know the facts. "Always be prepared to give an answer to everyone who asks you to give the reason for the hope that you have."

So, can you? Are you prepared? Can you give an answer?

Just the Facts, Ma'am, Just the Facts

"Dum di dum dum, dum di dum tum taaaa!" (No, I didn't get my fingers started at the wrong place on the keyboard. That's the theme from the old Dragnet TV show.) "The story you are about to see is true; the names have been changed to protect the innocent." Each time we heard the theme and the words of the introduction, we knew that "the city" would once again be a safe place for its citizens because Sergeant Friday and Officer Gannon were on the job. The bad guys didn't have a chance. There was one thing the sleuths of the small screen couldn't stand: fluff, unnecessary information. When they interviewed a victim or witness, they were very clear about what they were looking for, "Just the facts, ma'am, just the facts." Anything more than that would confuse and cloud the real issues.

It is no different when it comes to sharing our faith. We do not need to be able to relate to someone else the whole counsel of God, just the basics. This is easier for lay people to do than pastors. Pastors often try to include too much when they are speaking about Jesus and end up strangling people with information. (When you think about it, we pastors are always trying to say too much!) So, what do we need to know? What are the basics that we need to be able to communicate? Let's take a look.

The Basics

Because I am convinced that the most effective witnessing tool is not a slick, memorized Gospel presentation but rather the story of God at work in the lives of individuals, I am suggesting that you make use of seven basic statements that can be easily incorporated within the context of your life story. As you read through them, please notice how they flow from one to the other. There is a definite connection between each of the basics that moves forward the message of God's unconditional love in Jesus Christ.

Gospel Basic No. 1: God Loves Us Unconditionally

That sounds like such a simple statement, and yet many people have trouble understanding what it means and doesn't mean. The confusion shows itself in two very different ways:

1. Many people who live their lives apart from the Lord believe that God views them through the lenses of anger and judgment, not love. It is easy to understand how these feelings of guilt develop: Children are severely punished rather than appropriately disciplined. Lives are lived in fear that the "other shoe" is about to drop. Competitors in both work and play applaud when failures occur. With that mind-set, it is easy to ask, "Why wouldn't God be the same way? If others treat me as if I don't count, why should God be any different?" Unconditional love is a foreign concept in a world where most things are conditional, where there are no "free lunches," and where everything has a catch. When we are surrounded by the conditional love of "I'll love you as long as you love me and do what I say," it is little wonder that people have difficulty comprehending the love that God has for them in Jesus Christ.

2. Others have the opposite misconception. "Of course God loves me, he loves everyone. We're all going to heaven!" The first sentence is true. Oh, how I wish the second one was! God

does love everyone. He created us, he cares for us, Jesus died and rose again for us. The truth is that not everyone believes in Jesus. Not everyone will go to heaven. But that doesn't make God love them any less. The determining factor is whether or not, upon hearing the Gospel, we resist the Holy Spirit's work of creating faith in our lives.

Jesus' disciples came to grips with this truth when he asked, "Who do you say that I am?" (Matt. 16:13–20). The disciples reported the various popular views: "Some say John the Baptist; others say Elijah; and still others, Jeremiah or one of the prophets." That wasn't what Jesus asked. "But who do you say I am?" "Simon Peter answered, 'You are the Christ, the Son of the living God.' " That same question is asked in love of every individual, and there is still only one right answer!

God does, indeed, love everyone unconditionally, but not everyone will receive God's love by believing in the saving work of Jesus on the cross. Many keep themselves out of heaven, much to God's disappointment!

At Mount Olive, we frequently have opportunities to minister to individuals who have experienced very little love in their lives. Their lifestyle, attitude, and view of themselves make it difficult for them to ever imagine someone loving them unconditionally.

One woman I know used to be that way. She had a difficult time believing that anyone could love her, much less the God of all creation. It was through a long-term relationship that our congregation was able to show its love for her and enable her to discover what real love was all about. We became her example of love; up till then such examples had been few and far between. She had been raised in an abusive family, which greatly affected her image of a loving father. The Lord used unconditional love for her to communicate his love for her. Doors began to open; she became able to see that God desired her to have a full life, with him as an integral part of it. Jesus' words in John 10:10 showed her that someone actually loved her enough to care about her quality of life: "The thief comes only to steal and kill and destroy; I have come that they may have life, and have it to the full."

Since then, she has been baptized and continues to grow in her understanding of a loving God and Savior and the full life that he brings.

Gospel Basic No. 2: We Rebel against God's Love

We are rebels. Those who have difficulty believing that God could love them rebel by rejecting his love. Others, who are so sure that God loves everyone and that all roads lead to heaven, express their rebellion by refusing to acknowledge their sin and their need for forgiveness.

The Bible points out that it is our sin that keeps us from believing and receiving God's unconditional love. Rom. 3:23 says, "All have sinned and fall short of the glory of God." Is. 59:2 tells us, "Your iniquities have separated you from your God." In our state of rebellion, sin has such a strong grip on us that there is absolutely nothing that we can do to improve the situation on our own. We cannot solve the problem by ourselves because we are the problem!

Gospel Basic No. 3:
We Cannot Overcome Our Own Rebellion

The sad reality is that many people actually think that they can be good enough to break the hold sin and rebellion have on their lives and thereby earn God's favor and entrance to eternity. Our Lord has something else to say about that. Take a look at Eccl. 7:20, "There is not a righteous man on earth who does what is right and never sins." If it were left to us to clear up the problem of our own sin, none of us would stand a chance. God has a prerequisite for heaven: We must be perfect, sinless in every way. I don't know about you, but that basically disqualifies me. No amount of begging or pleading will change the reality of our blunders and rebellion.

California has the toughest car emissions laws in the nation. We have to. With the number of cars and the poor quality of our air, it's a wonder they let us drive at all! Before a vehicle's license registration can be renewed, it is required every other year to have a "smog check" at an officially licensed shop. If the car fails the test, repairs have to be made to bring it up to standard. (You can imagine how we Californians look forward to having our cars tested!)

We recently needed to have one of our cars "smogged." Kathy had been after me to get it done for several weeks so that we could send the registration in on time and not pay a penalty. During the week that the registration was due, I decided that it was time to act. So one morning I announced that it was Smog Check Day and that I would take the car in later. That afternoon, while Kathy was at the store and Andrew was still at school, I grabbed Timmy, our one-year-old, and headed to the smog check station.

I couldn't believe that there was an empty parking lot. There was usually a long wait; I was sure they must be closed. The shop was open, and the mechanic told me he could have me in and out in 20 minutes. I was thrilled! I even had a $4 off coupon. We would probably beat Kathy back home. True to his promise, 20 minutes later I was informed that I was the proud owner of a smog certificate; my car had passed. I presented my coupon, paid the balance of $30, and headed home.

Timmy and I were playing on the floor by the time his mother came home. I was rather pleased with myself, and she didn't even know what I had done. Before I could share my success, she began to speak.

"I'm sorry!"

"Sorry? For what?"

"I'm sorry that I took the car that you needed to have smogged!"

My self-righteous pleasure disappeared instantly. Now I had to tell her that I had taken the wrong car and that we were $30 poorer.

She was excited!

I had had the same car smogged only three months earlier. I forgot. My suggestion that "it is nice to know that the car works so well" was not well received. (Do other husbands do stupid things like this, too?)

My phone call to the smog-check station was not fruitful. I tried to explain what had happened. The mechanic laughed. No amount of begging or pleading could change the reality of my blunder. He said there was no excuse for brainlessness. (I really appreciated that one.) He tried to encourage me: "It's good to know your car works so well." I told him that I had already tried that one. His response?

"She didn't buy it, huh?"

We fail in the things of life all the time. Some of the things we do are brainless, others are willful acts of rebellion. Either way, there is no way to make them right. Our pitiful efforts are laughable; they always come up short.

What we really need is a spiritual smog check. That test can only be done by one person, our loving heavenly Father. The results? We fail every time. No tune-ups or minor repairs on our part will do the job. The only thing that will make the difference and bring acceptance is a complete life replacement, and God is the only one who can do that!

Gospel Basic No. 4:
Jesus Christ Is God's Solution to Our Rebellion

The Scriptures are really very clear: "There is one God and one mediator between God and men, the man Christ Jesus, who gave himself as a ransom for all men—the testimony given in its proper time" (1 Tim. 2:5–6). There is only one solution to our problem of sin; it is Jesus Christ. As the perfect God/Man who never rebelled, he comes as our mediator to stand between us and a perfect God who demands perfection from his creation.

I really like the word *ransom* that the Paul included in that verse. It fits our circumstances perfectly. We were held hostage by our sin. We were under the control and influence of a force that never meant good for us, only harm. It's as if we were tied up, unable to move, unable to help ourselves.

The story of Maximillian Kolbe never fails to come to mind when I think about Jesus' work of ransom. In 1941, Kolbe, a Franciscan priest, was tossed into a Nazi concentration camp because of his faith. Later that year, a prison escape occurred. Every time that happened, in order to ensure that others would not try the same thing, the commandant would order 10 prisoners killed for every one that escaped. They were selected at random, to be taken to a cell where they would starve to death.

Ten names were called. One of the 10, Gajowniczek, began to cry. He sobbed that he had a wife and children.

At that moment, something happened that was not allowed; a man pushed his way through the rows of prisoners until he stood before the officer; it was Kolbe.

"I want to die in the place of this prisoner. He has a wife and children, he is young and strong. I am old and worth nothing to you."

A stunned officer asked, "Who are you?"

"A Catholic priest."

The rows of prisoners and guards became awkwardly quiet in response to the strange request. The request was granted.

Maximillian Kolbe lived the longest of the 10. He did not die from starvation, he died only after the camp doctor injected him with a lethal medication. The ransom was paid by someone else, and Gajowniczek was spared.

That's what Jesus did, only he didn't die for just one person. He died for all the people who have lived or ever will. He paid the death penalty we deserve. He experienced the full reality of hell, complete separation from God, when, on the cross, he cried out, "My God, my God, why have you forsaken me?"

Wow, that's unconditional love!

Gospel Basic No. 5: God's Unconditional Love Brings Us Forgiveness and Peace through Jesus

Through Jesus, God shows us his unconditional love by bringing forgiveness and peace to the point where it is offered as a reality in our lives. When Jesus pays the penalty, the prisoners (that's us) are offered freedom and restored to life. God gives us the promise of forgiveness for our past failures and for the ones we have yet to commit. He offers us peace in place of the conflict that we continue to promote. In Eph. 1:7–8, the apostle Paul makes it clear that freedom and peace can be found in only one place, in Jesus Christ.

> In him we have redemption through his blood, the forgiveness of sins, in accordance with the riches of God's grace that he lavished on us with all wisdom and understanding.

The need for freedom and peace is very real. It is needed because our world is so full of conflict. Conflict occurs at home, at work, on foreign battlefields, in crack houses, in relationships, everywhere. No one is immune, everyone is affected.

We hear loud public outcries in places like Tiananmen Square, along the Berlin Wall, and in the halls of the Kremlin. But if we listen carefully, we will also hear the cry for freedom and peace in the deep recesses of individual human hearts. You see, it is not enough to just "give peace a chance" in streets of Jerusalem, where Arabs and Jews struggle to live side by side, or in the villages of South Africa, where apartheid divides and dehumanizes individuals. Real peace and freedom happens inside! It begins in a relationship with Jesus. When the quest for freedom and peace occurs apart from Jesus, it can bring only an incomplete, temporary physical relief. The forgiveness and peace that God offers through Jesus is lasting. It is not for a few only, it is for all. The problem? Not everyone will experience it, because not everyone will believe and trust in Jesus alone for their salvation.

Gospel Basic No. 6:
Trust in Jesus Alone As Our Personal Savior

Trust! Now there's a word you don't hear every day. If you were to believe everything that you see on TV's talk shows, you'd have to wonder if any relationship today includes trust as an important and valuable ingredient. When it comes to the relationship between us and our God, as expressed in faith, it is critical. The thing that trips up a lot of people is the big difference between believing in something and trusting in it. Without God, we can do neither. Allow me to give you an updated story from the Scriptures as evidence.

Jesus met a well-to-do young man who had everything going for him. He drove a red 4×4 chariot (all up-and-coming baby boomers dream of driving a family sized 4×4), bought his robes from Neiman-Marcus, wore handmade Italian sandals, and frequented the newest and best sushi bar in town. He had life by the tail, and he was swinging it! He believed in God, knew his catechism, and could recite the appropriate answers. (Sound like someone you know?)

> Jesus answered, "If you want to be perfect, go, sell your possessions and give to the poor, and you will have treasure in heaven. Then come, follow me." When the young man heard this, he went away sad, because he had great wealth. (Matt. 19:21–22)

You see, there is a difference between believing and trusting. The Bible tells us that even the demons believe (James 2:19), but they certainly do not trust in Jesus. In the case of the rich young man, he believed in God. He even seemed to have some intellectual knowledge about God. He did not trust. He wanted to retain control of his life.

As long as we retain control of our lives, we are trusting in ourselves to solve the problems of sin that separate us from our God, and we will fail every time. Our trust must be directed to Jesus' work of faithfulness and the ransom that he paid; it will happen no other way. And as his Spirit enables us to trust the reality of salvation, forgiveness and peace are realized.

Gospel Basic No. 7: God's Grace Enables Us to Live as Obedient Children Who Can Say No to Sin

By God's grace we place our faith in Jesus, and God gives us the power to become his children! It really is incredible when you think about it: a new life, a new identity, a new name (Christian), a new elder brother (Jesus), a new way of life. All ours—not because we deserve any of it, but because the God of all creation who sent his Son to be our Savior loves us. What is the result?

A new way of life!

My teenage years were no different from anyone else's. I did get into trouble enough to keep me in the dog house more times than I wanted, but then maybe you've already figured that out. Remember the line Moms and Dads always use? (I can't imagine that it was too different in your home.) "As long as you live in this house, you are going to live the way we do." Most of the time I did pretty good, but there were times when I didn't live up to being a Gibson. But the older I got, the more it mattered to me. I wanted to bring honor to my folks and be obedient because of my love for them, not just so I would stay out of trouble, which didn't hurt either.

When God enables us to believe and trust in Jesus as our Savior and Lord, we become part of his family. He adopts us as his children. The story and heritage of God and all of his family become ours and, with them, the opportunity and power to live obedient lives in a way that brings honor and glory to him.

Why do we do it? Why do we want to live a life of obedience through Spirit-powered faith? So we can stay out of trouble? Because we are afraid of the other option, hell?

No!

The reason is our great love for what he has done for us. God's gift of faith enables us to live lives that exchange our old sinful ways for a new life in Jesus Christ. Saint Paul explains it wonderfully in 2 Cor. 5:15. "He died for all, that those who live should no longer live for themselves but for him who died for them and was raised again."

I remember the day vividly. It was the day our youngest son, Timmy, came into our lives. It took place in the delivery room of a hospital immediately following his birth. There was so much excitement, tears and laughter. It was wonderful and at the same time bittersweet. Kathy and I were gaining a son. The birth mother was making the ultimate sacrifice; she was giving her son to us. A new life, a gift of love, was entrusted to our care. That day we assumed a responsibility to fulfill the commitment she had made when she so lovingly placed the crying 9-pound, 2-ounce baby into our arms and into our lives. Our lives could never be the same again.

God did that, too!

He gave up his Son to us so that we might have a new life. It was an act of love that brought about our adoption. It brings to us a wonderful responsibility to live our lives in a manner that gives praise to him in response to the commitment that he made to us with his ultimate gift.

I Love to Tell the Story!

There is nothing new in the basics we have just reviewed. Children and adults have been learning the basics in a variety of ways for a lot of years. But telling the old, old story of Jesus and his love becomes wonderfully new every time it is shared. It is exciting, and it is life changing. The old, old story will continue to do its work, but it will work best when it is a story that we know and treasure with all of our heart. It needs to become so second nature that it flows from one basic point to the next, painting the wonderful picture of Jesus and his unconditional love.

When ball players arrive at training camp, there is a critical emphasis on learning and re-learning the fundamentals of the game. In the heat of the athletic event, players do not have time to think about the basics. Regular review will enable their play to happen naturally, almost without thought. When the team takes the field, even the casual observer would be amazed that there are so many varieties of plays. We watch quarterbacks change plays at the line of scrimmage. Pitchers shake off signals from their catchers until they get the right pitch, while the fielders are adjusting their position in anticipation of where that pitch might be hit. Half-court offenses go into effect simply because the point guard in basketball calls the play by making a hand motion. Why can it happen so smoothly, effortlessly? Because the basics have become second nature.

The basics of witnessing need to become second nature too! It will make a profound difference in your witnessing if you will learn them. Don't just rely upon your previous training. For many that may have been a long time ago. Own them for yourself, make the truths of God's plan of salvation part of your story. If you do, you will be able to speak about them with ease and authority.

I am continually amazed when I see an expert in her field speak about the work she does. She is able to take complex issues and offer them in a manner that simpletons like me can understand. This is possible because she knows her subject matter so well that she is able to make the jump from the theoretical to the real. She can make the transition from training camp to the field where our life's stories seldom slow down enough to consider the fundamentals.

So, call for a time out. Make an appointment with yourself to learn the basics. Some day soon your conversation with a friend is going to develop to the point where the "stuff" of the Gospel needs to be shared. Be ready to give an account of the hope that is in you.

"Ladies and Gentleman, it's time to return to the basics. This is the Gospel!"

Onto the Field

1. Make memory cards, writing each of the seven basics of the Gospel on 3 × 5 cards. Copy an accompanying Scripture verse on the other side. Carry them with you. Put them in your purse, on the dashboard of your car, on the mirror in the bathroom at home. Learn them, learn them, learn them. Know the basics so well that you don't hesitate when using them.

2. Identify the parts of your story that illustrate each of the fundamentals. Consider how your story can provide a contemporary context for these basics. Consider using a tape recorder to practice telling your story, inserting the appropriate basics. Listen to the recording, critique yourself. Do it again until it is natural. Then go forth with confidence knowing that you are becoming equipped, not only to communicate the basics within the context of your story, but able to make changes and variations whenever they are needed.

Chapter 5

"Low, I Am with You Always"

On a long, hot summer afternoon, there is not much to do when you have grazed your fill, chewed your cud, and enjoyed a cool drink of water, that is, of course, assuming that you're a cow! Two rather heavy milk producers found themselves in just that situation. As a result, they decided to spend the afternoon standing lazily along a fence bordering a busy road, watching the cars go by. After a while, a tanker trailer full of milk drove past. The trailer had this printed large on its side: "Our Milk Is Pasteurized, Homogenized, Vitamins Added." After a few moments of thought, one cow turned to the other, "Kind of makes you feel inadequate, doesn't it?"

Cracked Pots

There are no people alive who have not felt inadequate and overwhelmed when it comes to sharing their faith in Jesus Christ. We are privileged to carry the story of the greatest event in the history of the world to other people, and, when you think about it, that is extremely overwhelming. It should humble us to realize that our witnessing will affect the eternal well-being of people. It is truly amazing that God would choose you and me to be his messengers in our world. What an honor!

When I first became a pastor, I was blessed to be teamed up with a pastor who had more than 50 years of experience. I remember one Sunday morning, immediately before we were to begin worship, expressing to him my uncertainty about my message. His response has stayed with me: "God did not choose perfect messengers through which he communicates his perfect message. He chose 'cracked pots' like you and me! You'll be just fine."

Cracked pots. I love it! Take a look at 2 Cor. 4:5–7.

> We do not preach ourselves, but Jesus Christ as Lord, and ourselves as your servants for Jesus' sake. For God, who said, "Let light shine out of darkness," made his light shine in our hearts to give us the light of the knowledge of the glory of God in the face of Christ. But we have this treasure in jars of clay to show that this all-surpassing power is from God and not from us.

If the messengers (that's us, jars of clay) were as perfect as the treasure (the saving work of Jesus), the message could become obscured. God chose jars of clay, human beings with human frailties and sin, to make unmistakably clear that the message of forgiveness and full life originates from him and his power, not from us. The apostle

Paul adds some additional insight, this time from 1 Cor. 2:1–5.

> When I came to you, brothers, I did not come with eloquence or superior wisdom as I proclaimed to you the testimony about God. For I resolved to know nothing while I was with you except Jesus Christ and him crucified. I came to you in weakness and fear, and with much trembling. My message and my preaching were not with wise and persuasive words, but with a demonstration of the Spirit's power, so that your faith might not rest on men's wisdom, but on God's power.

While Saint Paul obviously felt overwhelmed and inadequate, he did not let that keep him from acting. He did not stop sharing the Gospel. His fear did not paralyze him. Instead, it made him realize how precious the message is and how, through his imperfection, God's power to change lives would be expressed clearly.

So if feeling overwhelmed and inadequate is normal, why do we let those feelings stop us from witnessing? Many people will answer, "I just don't feel led to witness." The reality of the situation is that frequently the only "led" we feel is the "lead" in the seat of our pants. Most of our excuses are weak. Few hold water.

Why, really, is there so little action on our part? Because a battle is being fought, a spiritual struggle so quiet and tricky that we hardly realize that we are the battleground as well as the prize.

Our enemy, whom the Bible calls Satan, does not want people to know Jesus as their Savior. To accomplish this, he has taken on the task of discouraging you and me, leading us to believe that our inadequacies make us incapable of witnessing. He wants to convince us that, as witnesses, we are all alone and that we are certainly not qualified to be effective. Or, he convinces us that since we are uncomfortable doing this, God doesn't expect anything of us. Whatever approach Satan uses, he works very hard to take our eyes off the God of all creation who can and does communicate his power through us.

Allow me to take us to a time long ago, to a place called Ophrah (no, not *Oprah,* the TV talk show) where a young man named Gideon learned that God's power was greater than anything and that God could work, even through him (Judges 6–7).

Gideon: He Can't Mean Me!

It wasn't an easy time in which to live. Most of Israel had forgotten to make God the central part of their lives. And if that wasn't bad enough, Israel also had to deal with some pretty nasty neighbors. It seemed that every time these neighbors, the Midianites, got hungry, they would send a little raiding party over the border to pick up dinner. Judges 6:5–6 explains, "They came up with their livestock and their tents like swarms of locusts. It was impossible to count the men and their their camels; they invaded the land to ravage it. Midian so impoverished the Israelites that they cried out to the LORD for help." (Maybe I did understate the problem just a little!)

The Lord provided the people an answer to their problem, a rather average guy named Gideon. "The angel of the LORD came and sat down under the oak in Ophrah that belonged to Joash the Abiezrite, where his son Gideon was threshing wheat in a winepress to keep it from the Midianites. When the angel of the LORD appeared to Gideon, he said, 'The LORD is with you, mighty warrior' " (Judges 6:11–12).

"Mighty warrior?" That was quite a compliment, but Gideon was certain the heavenly messenger must be thinking of someone else. You see, Gideon wasn't exactly the boldest one in his family. He was, after all, threshing wheat in a winepress, an enclosed place, for fear the Midianites might spot him. So he sets about to use his inadequacies as reason not to act. " 'But Lord,' Gideon asked, 'how can I save Israel? My clan is the weakest in Manasseh, and I am the least in my family.' " Gideon knew his limitations. The job description overwhelmed him. There had to be a way out.

What to do? Maybe a sign would help him know for sure. He needed more than a little confidence before he would risk sticking his neck out and getting it cut off. He set food before the Lord, and the angel touched it with the tip of his staff and it vaporized. God had his attention!

That's when things really got hot at the border. A multinational force was coming together to conduct the "Mother of All Battles." It was time for Gideon to go into action. He did. He offered God yet another chance to change his mind and pick someone else to do the job, or else to guarantee victory in advance.

> Gideon said to God, "If you will save Israel by my hand as you have promised—look, I will place a wool fleece on the threshing floor. If there is dew only on the fleece and all the ground is dry, then I will know that you will save Israel by my hand, as you said." And that is what happened. Gideon rose early the next day; he squeezed the fleece and wrung out the dew—a bowlful of water. (Judges 6:36–38)

Now you might think that would be enough to convince ol' Gideon that God meant to do exactly what he promised. Wrong! Gideon decided to give the Lord one final chance. "He still must be confused; he can't mean me!"

> Then Gideon said to God, "Do not be angry with me. Let me make just one more request. Allow me one more test with the fleece. This time make the fleece dry and the ground covered with dew." That night God did so. Only the fleece was dry; all the ground was covered with dew. (Judges 6:39–40)

Gideon was locked in. The Lord had backed him to the wall! It was time for action. The least he could do was make sure the battle wasn't a rout by gathering as many men as he could to serve in his army. The men came in huge numbers; things were looking up.

> The LORD said to Gideon, "You have too many men for me to deliver Midian into their hands. In order that Israel may not boast against me that her own strength has saved her, announce now to the people, 'Anyone who trembles with fear may turn back and leave Mount Gilead.' " (Judges 7:2–3)

That invitation sounds like announcing to passengers about to board the *Titanic* that the ship is guaranteed to sink and anyone concerned about it should turn around and go home. I'll bet Gideon's heart sank! "So twenty-two thousand men left, while ten thousand remained" (Judges 7:3). And just when Gideon is getting used to this reduction in force, new orders come down from headquarters: "There's still too many; you've got to get rid of some more!"

I think God smiles at us a lot. I'm convinced that he enjoys his creation, and I think that he was having a little fun with Gideon. Please allow me to fill in the spaces between a few lines and verses of Judges 7.

"Gideon, remember all that silly stuff you had me do with the fleece so you would be sure you'd win the war? Well, it's my turn. Here's what I want you to do. Take your guys down to the water and have them drink. (Don't laugh, Gideon. A wet fleece smells a lot worse than a wet soldier!) The men who drink by cupping their hands in the water and holding them to their mouths are the ones you want. They are the watchful ones; they will serve you the best. Those who put their faces into the water like dogs and lap up their water, those send back to camp."

9,700 men obviously never listened when their mothers taught them manners. They were sent home. How are your math skills? Have you figured out how many are left of the original 32,000 man army? A whopping 300!

When you hear what Gideon handed out as weapons, you might think that the whole experience had affected him emotionally. On the surface his choice of armor looked like a big mistake, trumpets, clay jars, and torches! (Now there's a great way to build confidence in the rank and file.) But don't overlook the results. They won! The Lord confused the enemy, blinded them with the light from the torches, and they turned upon each other.

God was working out his plan all along. He knew exactly what he was doing, which included asking a simple, hesitant, everyday kind of guy like Gideon to accomplish his goals. When Gideon faced and admitted his limitations and then put his trust in God, Gideon was at his strongest. The story of Gideon is the story of the Lord working through a "cracked pot," just as he will work through you and me to get his Gospel out to others.

The Holy Spirit: the 10th Man

In baseball it's the 10th man; in football it's the 12th man. In both cases it is the crowd, the fans. When the fans get involved in the game, cheering, encouraging the players, and booing the umpires (that's one of my favorite parts), it makes a difference for the players. That's what God does for us.

When he commands us to witness, he makes a difference by giving us the person of the Holy Spirit as our 10th man. We have his absolute promise that we are never alone, that he will guide us, encourage and comfort us, not only when we obey him, but even when we fail or falter.

I like the story about the pastor who needed to make airline reservations for a flight to the Orient. Obviously nervous, he began to question the travel agent.

"How long a flight is this?"

"Oh, about 16 hours."

"Sixteen hours, huh? Ah, ah . . . Well, will any meals be served?"

"Several. You're going to be in the air a long time."

"This flight goes over the ocean, doesn't it?"

"That's the quickest way to get there!"

"How high will the plane be flying?"

"Somewhere around 35,000 feet."

"Oh! (Pause.) Will there be a movie?"

"Sure, on the round trip you'll have two, one on the way there and one on the way back. What's the matter, Pastor? You're afraid, aren't you?"

"No, no, I'm ah, ah . . . I'm not afraid at all."

"You're afraid, I can tell! I work with people all the time who are afraid to travel long distances by air. Come on, admit it. I can tell, you're afraid."

"No, really I'm, I'm not . . . "

"Pastor, doesn't God say in the Bible, 'I am with you always' ?"

"No, what he says in the Bible is, 'LOW, I am with you always.' Not at 35,000 feet in the air!"

It's great! The God of all creation is with you every moment of your life. You are never alone, whether you are walking on the ground or sitting in an airplane cruising at hundreds of miles an hour, tens of thousands of feet in the air. And you are never alone when you share your faith with someone else.

The Holy Spirit brings to us more than his presence, encouragement, and guidance. He brings power to us. The Greek word for power is *dunamis,* the root of our English word, dynamite. The Spirit of God in you is a powerful agent of change. He changed you when he made you a believer in Jesus as your Savior. When you are witnessing, he works through his Word to change the life of the person you are talking to. And he gives you the power to help you witness in spite of your inadequacies. Don't overlook Paul's dynamite in Phil. 4:13, "I can do everything through him who gives me strength." That word—*everything*—leaves no room for limitations. It is truly all-inclusive. It even applies to witnessing!

Onto the Field

God has provided the power to overcome the feelings of inadequacy that keep us from doing the work of witnessing, of entering into the battle for the hearts and minds of people who do not know him as Savior and Lord. The presence of the Holy Spirit in our lives has given us all the armor and weaponry we'll ever need. When was the last time you put yours on? I once saw an advertisement in a newspaper that read as follows:

FOR SALE: One suit of Christian armor; hardly ever worn.

Clever, isn't it? Unfortunately, it is also true in far too many cases. Let's reverse the trend and take the time daily to put on our armor. Begin by reading Eph. 6:10–20. As you read the passage, identify the various items that will equip you to stand firm.

1. verse 14
2. verse 15
3. verse 16
4. verse 17

5. verse 17 (A clue: the only offensive weapon)

6. verses 18–20

Commit daily to prayerfully "putting on" each element of your armor. It's there to use, don't let it rust! Don't allow your inadequacies to keep you from marching forward.

Chapter 6

Why Am I Afraid?

I hate sailboats! My brother has a beautiful one docked on San Francisco Bay, a gorgeous thing with teakwood interior, polished brass, and billowing sails. It's gorgeous, that is, until it starts to heel over in a breeze. Now please understand that I'm not particularly afraid of boats or the water. I just have an aversion to being in the cockpit where the gunwale has now become the floor and the ocean is rushing by only inches below my feet.

One day when we were out in Doug's boat, both he and my wife took great glee in my terror. Both recommended that I go below until I felt more comfortable. I thought that was a lousy idea; I wanted to be on deck where I could jump off should the vessel capsize. The other thing causing my consternation was the realization that our sailing water was also a major port for such insignificant vessels as aircraft carriers, tankers, and huge cargo ships. My muscles hurt for a week after holding them tense all those hours.

In contrast to my moments of terror in a sailboat, I happen to like slamming through the water in a power boat. All that force at my disposal thrills me. So why am I afraid of one and not the other? I think I've got it figured out.

When I'm in a sailboat, I am at the mercy of the wind and waves, the elements around me. I am not in control (at least it appears that way to me). Sailboats do not seem stable. They tip and are uncertain. (I know, I know. Sailboats are supposed to be much safer than motorized craft, but tell that to my nerves and you won't gain a hearing.) In my mind a motorized boat is under my control. It feels stable, and I feel much less vulnerable.

Have you figured out where I'm going with all of this? Most of our fears are based upon a personal perception of vulnerability. We are uncertain about doing the work of witnessing, because we do not always feel in control. The person to whom we are speaking guides much of the conversation. We think, "If I can simply avoid having to witness, then I do not have to worry about being afraid." The problem is that many people will not hear our story of faith unless we learn to overcome our concerns.

I'll let you in on a little secret: I've only been on a sailboat one time. "So," you ask, "how can you decide that you hate sailboats after only one try?" You've got me there! It is silly to base a decision purely on one experience, and yet most Christians have made a similar decision about sharing their faith without having really given it a try! I'll make a deal with you. You put some effort into sharing your faith with someone you care about over a period of time, and I'll go out on my brother's boat again. Then we'll compare notes. If we are truly honest with ourselves, we will have to admit that most of our fears are based on ignorance. We really have little upon which to base them.

Overcoming Fear: Try Walking on Water

Jesus and the disciples had had a busy day!

Waiting on people and busing tables for a crowd of 5,000 men plus women and children was no easy task, even if the food was prepared miraculously. When dinner was over and the place settings were cleared, Jesus told the disciples to go ahead of him to the city of Gennesaret. That meant a boat ride across Lake Galilee, which wasn't a big deal to these guys. A number of them were fishermen, and they knew this lake like the back of their hand.

As it turned out, that night they had an opportunity to put all of their sailing ability to the test in the midst of a rough storm. When things were getting frustrating, and they were not making much headway against the wind and waves, the strangest thing happened, something that never before had occurred. Someone was coming toward them on the water, walking!

Now, we know it was Jesus, but at the time they weren't too sure. The superstition of the day warned that demons and ghosts lived in bodies of water, and a rough sea was regarded as evidence of the anger of these specters. It's no wonder they thought a ghost was coming toward them.

Jesus, not wanting them to be frightened, called out to them, "Take courage! It is I. Don't be afraid." (That's easy for Jesus to say!) On this side of the experience, we wonder how any of the disciples had trouble believing it was Jesus. After all, they should have recognized his voice.

But some of the disciples had a sailing background. They knew that when people stepped out onto the water they were not supposed to walk, they were supposed to sink. It was contrary to their understanding of the way the world functions. Impossible!

Peter, however, decided to test the water (sorry for the pun). "Lord, if it's you, tell me to come to you on the water" (Matt. 14:28). Look closely at that verse and you'll discover that Peter was hedging his bet. If it wasn't Jesus, he was safe, he wouldn't be asked to walk on the water. If it was Jesus, well, that was a different story. He was committed! He had said it loud enough for all of the rest to hear. There was no way he could back down. His only hope was that the same miraculous power that had fed all those thousands the day before and that was keeping Jesus from sinking would also make a difference for him.

"Come," Jesus said.

This was beyond anything Peter had ever experienced. Before he knew it, that rugged fisherman was out of the boat and walking on the water. All his experience told him he wasn't supposed to be able to do this, and yet he was!

Then things started to go wrong. Peter remembered the waves and the wind and his world view that knew for certain that walking on water was impossible. As soon as he started focusing on the perceived difficulties and took his eyes off of Jesus, he sank!

We can hardly miss the lesson for witnessing this story offers: God can and does enable us to share our faith in circumstances outside our comfort zone. The key, obviously, is to keep our eyes focused on Jesus. As long as we do that, we can walk, we can do the work of witnessing. However, once we take our eyes off him and start concentrating on all of our internal inadequacies and fears, not to mention all the hostile surrounding circumstances, we become paralyzed, and sinking is not far behind.

Winning the Battle of Fear

1. Name Your Fears

Let's be honest! You've got inadequacies and I've got inadequacies. As we discovered earlier from Paul's counsel to the Corinthians, acknowledging our inadequacie, is an important step when we are sharing the message of Jesus. It's also imperative that we give our fear a name. See how Paul did it. "When I came to you, brothers, I did not come with eloquence or superior wisdom as I proclaimed to you the testimony about

God. . . . I came to you in weakness and fear, and with much trembling. . . . so that your faith might not rest on men's wisdom, but on God's power" (1 Cor. 2:1, 3, 4).

Our feelings of fear about witnessing serve an important purpose. They keep us honest. They keep us focused on God's empowering help. We experience his promise that when we are weak he will make us strong. Name your fears one by one, so that Christ's power comes to rest on you.

2. You Know the Subject Matter

Do you fear you won't know what to say when you try to witness? God has never asked us to talk about something we do not know. We have the privilege of telling our story, how the Lord is involved in our lives. I've never met a person who wasn't able to talk about himself. When we're telling our story, we can speak with confidence; we know the subject matter pretty well.

3. Focus on the Need

Do you fear witnessing because of the circumstances? Let me show you how to handle that fear. It was my first day of hospital calls during my pastoral internship. My vicarage supervisor did a great job of guiding me through all the hospitals and modeling effective hospital ministry. Everything went fine until the last visit of the day.

The patient was an elderly gentleman. Before his hospitalization, he had been a resident of a convalescent home where he had not been very cooperative; he didn't like to change his socks. It turned out that he had been hiding an infection which eventually became an open ulcer where his ankle used to be, only we didn't know it!

As we were talking and praying, his doctor came in to check his ulcerated foot, which was wrapped in bandages. I tried to be relaxed and cool, but this was awful. While it certainly wasn't visually appealing, it carried with it the extra impact of the horrible smell of rotting flesh. After our visit, we stood in the hall and chatted with the doctor.

"I don't know how you guys could stand that. (This was the doctor talking!) It's one of the worst open ulcers I've ever seen."

My vicarage pastor responded with great bravery, "Oh, I've seen lots of tough cases. I used to be an ambulance driver for a rescue squad."

It was my turn. "I don't know about you guys, but this is bothering me a lot."

I couldn't understand why, but when they looked at me they had such panicked expressions on their faces, at least until I passed out. I came to as they were walking me back and forth in the hallway, trying desperately to keep me from falling over.

Great! My first day of hospital ministry and I pass out! 6'4", 230 pounds and I have a glass stomach. Pastors spend lots of time in hospitals. What was I going to do? How would I be able to minister at the bedside of someone who was ill when I felt like getting sick myself?

Our conversation on the way home did wonders.

Suggested my supervising pastor, "Just focus on the person and his need, not on the circumstances, and it won't happen again."

It made sense. I have since learned to care so much about the person with whom I am ministering that I am able to look past the tubes and bottles, bells and whistles, to see the hurt and the need. As a result, I haven't fainted in a hospital again.

It works in witnessing, too. I have been sharing my faith with others for a long time, and I still get scared. What if they reject me? What happens if they tell me to take a long walk on a short pier? Now I know the answers to all of these questions, and yet it doesn't mean that I'm not bothered by them; I have just learned to push past them. The thing that makes the difference is my motivation: I want my friend to spend eternity with me in heaven. The hurt and the need that must be addressed is not whether I'll be rejected. Instead of focusing on my fears about how well I'm doing, I concentrate on whether or not she trusts in Jesus Christ alone for her salvation. When I learn to focus on the other person's eternal needs, I am able to look past my fears and do the sharing that is needed.

4. Faith Is Spelled R-I-S-K

Witnessing is an act of faith. Acting in faith always calls for risk. It is risky to trust God for something that, were he not in it, would be destined for failure. There is a big difference between having the head knowledge that something is true and believing it with all your heart and mind, believing it so strongly that you take the risk of acting on it.

When the time came for Peter to act, he had to pick up his feet, swing his legs over the gunwale and step down onto the water. The time for bravado was over. The moment called for action. Faith was being spelled in capital letters, R-I-S-K! "Now faith is being sure of what we hope for and certain of what we do not see." (Heb. 11:1)

The time comes in witnessing when we have to go into action. Sure, it's fun to sit around reading and talking about sharing our faith, because talk is safe. We don't have to do anything about it. But if we are going to accomplish the work of proclaiming God's ministry of reconciliation, we must face our fears and take the risk.

To help us do that, our Lord has given us these and many other wonderful promises:

I can do everything through him who gives me strength. (Phil. 4:13)

You will receive power when the Holy Spirit comes on you; and you will be my witnesses in Jerusalem, and in all Judea and

Samaria, and to the ends of the earth. (Acts 1:8)

On my account you will be brought before governors and kings as witnesses to them and to the Gentiles. But when they arrest you, do not worry about what to say or how to say it. At that time you will be given what to say, for it will not be you speaking, but the Spirit of your Father speaking through you. (Matt. 10:18–20)

Your fear is real and maybe it's big. God's promises are bigger. He will help you with your fear. So name it. Name each fear. Put one of God's promises over each one, and climb out of your safe seat. It's time to step onto the water of witnessing and, for the sake of the Gospel and the eternal well-being of someone for whom Christ died, risk!

How do you spell faith?

Onto the Field

When I take my eyes off the Lord, fear surfaces surprisingly quickly. It worked that way for the apostle Peter, and I'll bet it's true for you. To keep our eyes on Jesus, we must put our fears into their proper perspective. Ask yourself a few "perspective questions":

Is God bigger than my fear? Is he willing to do whatever it takes to make me an effective witness? Has he given me his Spirit to empower me as a witness? Is he calling me out of the boat of my fears and onto the water where people need his gift of salvation? If I begin to sink, will he put out his hand and lift me up?

If you answered yes to these "perspective" questions, I have one final one for you. What are you waiting for? It's time to step out of the boat and join God in the work!

Chapter 7

Being Real

It was truly amazing! He had been out of work only two days and he had already found a job that interested him. The City Zoo had openings on their staff. He loved animals; at one time he had even wanted to be a veterinarian. When he arrived at the zoo, he discovered that the position was still available. The personnel director offered this job description.

"Our gorilla died the other day, and we can't afford to replace him. So, we're looking for someone who would be willing to dress up in a gorilla suit and spend the day in the gorilla cage entertaining zoo visitors. Are you interested?"

This had to be the strangest job he had ever heard of, but he was out of work and the bills had to be paid.

"Sure, I'll take the job."

Thirty minutes later, wearing a new suit, he settled into his own office, under a tree in the gorilla pit. When the zoo opened and people started to gather along the railing, he discovered that every time he moved the people would respond with excitement. (This was fun.) He beat his chest; the crowd applauded. He climbed onto the swing; people started laughing. This really got him going, they loved him! He began to swing, pushing higher and higher each time the crowd cheered. During one of his swings something happened. He lost his grip, flew over the wall of the gorilla pit, and landed in the front yard of his neighbor, the lion.

As he regained his senses he realized that the lion had placed a big paw on the back of his neck. It was time for the charade to end.

"Help me! I'm not really a gorilla, I'm just a person dressed like one. Someone get me out of here."

A harsh whisper suddenly emerged from the lion, "Be quiet, or we'll both lose our jobs!"

Few people's work requires them to be so phony that they have to put on a gorilla suit before heading to the office. And yet, most people are willing, from time to time, to misrepresent themselves in order to enjoy a better image in the eyes of others. When the need is there, phoniness is as easy to slip into as a dress or a pair of pants!

In contrast, there is certainly nothing phony about God, and there should be nothing phony about those who are representing him to an unbelieving world. Misrepresenting ourselves is one of the quickest ways to disrupt the communication of God's Good News. In witnessing, phoniness is a terminal disease. The truth of God's love in Jesus Christ expects a truthful messenger. Witnessing requires us to be real!

When we think about sharing our faith with others, reminders that we are less than perfect quickly come to mind. While we certainly experience the wonderful blessings of God, the joy of forgiveness and the strength to live for him, our stories are also full of failure, sin, weakness, and our incredible ability to disappoint God and others without even trying. Along with these reminders of our imperfections comes the temptation to cover them up. "Mr. and Mrs. Perfect Holier-Than-Thou." You've heard the complaint; it is a favorite of unbelievers as they critique the lives of believers. Frequently, we deserve much of the negative press we receive. We make a really good effort at offering a picture of ourselves that tries to suggest that Christians are clean, shiny, and pure. A more accurate picture of Jesus' people is of sinners who have been cleansed and declared pure by the pure Son of God, Jesus Christ. The minute we allow ourselves to admit to others that we too are sinful people who are in regular need of forgiveness, we will be much more effective witnesses.

King David—the Pain of Becoming Real

The 11th and 12th chapters of 2 Samuel paint a tragic picture of the real life of a believer struggling with sin.

She was beautiful and, unknowingly, had his full attention. King David, after a restless afternoon rest, had left his bed for a stroll around the roof of his palace. For Bathsheba it was simply time for a bath.

"Who is that woman?"

"It's Bathsheba, the daughter of Eliam and wife of Uriah the Hittite."

"Get her for me!"

It was all so easy. It may have been "only" a one night stand but it brought forth a whole string of dramatic events. (That stuff God says about "what you sow you shall reap" makes a lot of sense.)

When the messenger from Bathsheba had left, David was stunned; he couldn't believe it. "Pregnant? She can't be pregnant. It'll ruin my life. God's bound to be upset, and it certainly isn't politically correct, either. What am I going to do?"

When the ideas came, they came fast.

"Quick, someone go to the battle front and get her husband, Uriah. Send him home so that he can sleep with his wife, and everyone will think that he's the father of the baby. No one will know it was me."

Every king should have such a dedicated soldier; Uriah would not allow himself the pleasure of his wife's company while his men had to sleep in open fields. Next night David tried again, this time getting Uriah drunk, but this man of rock-solid principles didn't budge. He slept with the rest of the palace servants and made the king look very bad.

This wasn't the way it was supposed to work. Plans A and B had failed. Plan C was all that was left; it was to be the final move of a desperate conspirator. "Put Uriah in the front line where the fighting is fiercest. Then withdraw from him so he will be struck down and die" (2 Sam. 11:15).

When the days of Bathsheba's mourning were over (probably a seven day period), she married David and bore him a son. On the surface it all looked so innocent, a happy couple with a new baby. But don't miss the last line of the chapter: "But the thing David had done displeased the LORD" (2 Sam. 11:27).

Enter Nathan, the trusted friend of the King, who told a story that finally brought David back to reality.

"There were two men in a certain town, one rich and the other poor. The rich man had a very large number of sheep and cattle, but the poor man had nothing except one little ewe lamb he had bought. He raised it, and it grew up with him and his children. It shared his food, drank from his cup, and even slept in his arms. It was like a daughter to him. Now a traveler came to the rich man, but the rich man refrained from taking one of his own sheep or cattle to prepare a meal for the traveler who had come to him. Instead, he took the ewe lamb that belonged to the poor man and prepared it for the one who had come to him." David burned with anger against the man and said to Nathan, "As surely as the LORD lives, the man who did this deserves to die! He must pay for that lamb four times over, because he did such a thing and had no pity." Then Nathan said to David, "You are the man!" (2 Sam. 12:1–7)

Gotcha!

The time for phoniness was over; it was time to be painfully real.

"I have sinned against the LORD."

Nathan replied, "The LORD has taken away your sin" (2 Sam. 12:13).

Bathsheba, Uriah, Nathan, and the infant that eventually died were all part of David's story. It wasn't a positive chapter in his life, but there it was, nevertheless. David could not change it, but it forever changed him. It required him to be honest with himself, his God, and those around him. His life became an example of the healing, forgiving power of the Savior, providing for us a real experience of another sinner, just like us, who needed and received forgiveness and restoration.

David is a great example of the many people in the Scriptures through whom God worked, showing us the importance of being real. Our Lord has lots of ways of bringing us to that point. The circumstances that he allows to occur in individual lives clears the way for the message of the Gospel to eternally affect the lives of others.

When we are willing to risk being real, our lives become examples, Cross Points, that provide a context for the Gospel that a fellow sinner will be able to understand. The negative stories of our lives are not to be celebrations of sin; rather, they point to the glorious forgiving power of Christ to change and heal lives.

Redemption, Not Escape

Everyone is always looking for a way out, a shortcut through life's problems; there's no such thing! King David knew it, so do we, deep down. Our struggles are for real, and they are here to stay. We can't change our past, any more than David could. What can change is the result of the struggle. Our lives do not have to end in defeat. Jesus said it clearly, "In this world you will have trouble. But take heart! I have overcome the world" (John 16:33).

Our faith stories tell about Jesus' work of redemption, not about our escape from sin. Salvation provides us with the opportunity to focus on what Jesus has done, not on how awful we have been. Jesus enables us to realize his gift of forgiveness on a daily basis as we repent of our sins, confess our failures, and hear his message of restoration. That's where real hope comes from. Read Rom. 5:1–5, and see Paul describe how we are moved from struggle to hope.

> Therefore, since we have been justified through faith, we have peace with God through our Lord Jesus Christ, through whom we have gained access by faith into this grace in which we now stand. And we rejoice in the hope of the glory of God. Not

only so, but we also rejoice in our sufferings, because we know that suffering produces perseverance; perseverance, character; and character, hope. And hope does not disappoint us, because God has poured out his love into our hearts by the Holy Spirit, whom he has given us.

Here are the REAL facts:

1. Sin and struggle are part of the reality of everyone's life. Pretending that they don't exist will never make them go away.

2. Jesus' death and resurrection offer forgiveness, restoration, and hope for every situation in our lives.

Knowing my sinfulness and the power of God to change my life enables me to identify with the needs of others. Admitting my hurts and failures helps me be sensitive to their struggles, and it also makes my witness believable and convincing. Since Jesus made a difference in my life by dying on a cross with my name on it, I know he can do the same for them.

Being a "real" witness for Jesus is a wonderful leveling factor. It keeps my spiritual feet on the ground, far away from the temptation to assume a "holier than thou" attitude. Keeping my focus on what Jesus has done for me, rather than on the "pearls of wisdom" that I have to share with an unbeliever, creates a line of communication through which the Gospel will move in a powerful way.

Real Hope in the Midst of Pain

She wasn't beautiful like Bathsheba, not now. Oh, she was in earlier days, I've seen the pictures. But then, those were the days of Mabel Palmberg's life before cancer.

She hurt. I could see it in her yellow, jaundiced face in the moments before she realized that I was there, standing in the doorway of her hospital room. It was the same every time I visited her. Always a smile. Always a blessing to the one who had come to minister to her.

The nurses didn't quite know what to do with Mabel. They certainly knew what to do *for* her; they had treated lots of terminal patients. They just didn't know what to do with *her*. Mabel brought a presence of love and hope to a space that should have been full of dread and fear. But fear didn't have any room in Mabel's life, because it was filled with Jesus!

She loved to talk about Jesus and her death and resurrection. That wasn't a conversation that was reserved for the preacher. It was the topic of conversation with everyone who came to visit or to offer medical care.

In the last weeks before her death, when the hospital could do no more for her, they moved her to a special care home. Few people who went into that building ever walked out. Mabel would be no exception.

The first time I visited her there was the last time I saw her alive. I guess I really did expect to see a change for the worse. Oh, she was sicker, but I was sure that she would be depressed. (Why not, I was. After all, this was the house of death.) Pain filled her face, but resurrection fell from her lips. Some things never change.

We celebrated Easter in January! (We don't have many funerals in our church!) Mabel had carefully told me how she wanted the service to be. Even when it hurt so bad, when it was difficult to talk, she wanted to make sure that every person who came was going to know her hope. They did. Their ears and hearts were wide open.

They heard of a real life, real struggles, and a real death. They also heard about a real Savior who comes to make a real difference in the lives of real people. They all were nodding their heads as I spoke. They knew Mabel. She had made sure that they knew her hope. It was all very, very real.

Onto the Field

Few passages of Scripture make an impact in my life like 1 John 1:8–10. It enables me to see the real me.

> If we claim to be without sin, we deceive ourselves and the truth is not in us. If we confess our sins, he is faithful and just and will forgive us our sins and purify us from all unrighteousness. If we claim we have not sinned, we make him out to be a liar and his word has no place in our lives.

Use this "Onto the Field" assignment as a time to work on being real. Reflect on your life with the Lord and the sins that continue to defeat you. Talk to God in prayer, acknowledge your sin, and ask for his forgiveness. His promise is constant, he will forgive you of your sins and purify you from all unrighteousness.

As you witness to others, you will have the opportunity to tell your faith story. That story includes the sins you have committed as well as the forgiveness you have received. What will you tell? Give careful thought to ways you can emphasize Jesus and minimize yourself. God wants your hearer to have the glorious experience of knowing the Savior, not how rotten you have been. It may help you think this through by writing (and, if necessary, rewriting) your ideas and thoughts.

Chapter 8

You've Got to Have a Game Plan

They were supposed to be playing catch, but it seemed like every ball went untouched. One of the kids would throw the ball and the other would chase it; the scenario repeated itself again and again. Multiply that by 15 ballplayers, and you have one of the great comic scenes of the year. If the balls had been hand grenades, half of the city of San Jose would have disappeared. Welcome to T-ball!

The ballfield was covered with 4- and 5-year-olds. Even though they were in the midst of a game (and I use that term very loosely), few were paying attention. Some were sitting in the dirt trying to untie the knots that held their gloves together, while others chased butterflies or stared at the vapor trails of jets flying overhead.

T-ball is definitely not meant to be a professional league. It is a place for beginners, where the "how to" is always more important than the score. The amazing thing is that in the midst of all the successes and mistakes of the game, learning actually takes place, growth occurs, and skills are acquired. Learning to play baseball, like many things in life, is "caught," not "taught."

The same thing holds true when it comes to learning how to share our faith. The purpose of this chapter is to "catch" witnessing by guiding you through the process of identifying the person with whom you will share your faith and developing a "game plan" to bring to that person the life-changing power of the Gospel. This is the T-ball chapter of witnessing, where the "how to" is more important than the score.

How Do I Begin?

Begin the same way the disciples did. John 1:35–51 tells us the story of the simple, yet powerful manner in which Jesus called the first disciples to follow him. Allow me to let you in on a secret. Every person mentioned in these verses followed Jesus as the result of a relationship with some other person or group.

First, John the Baptizer directed two of his disciples (one of them was Andrew) to Jesus: "Look, the Lamb of God!" (v. 35). The second relationship was a family tie. After finding out where Jesus was staying, Andrew ran to get his brother, Simon (Peter). Even though Jesus called Philip directly (v. 43), we learn that "Philip, like Andrew and Peter, was from the town of Bethsaida" (v. 44). Did hometown buddies introduce Philip to the Master? In like manner, Philip finds his friend, Nathanael, and brings him to Jesus. The Lord used four interconnected relationships to draw people to himself! Examining this network of relationships will help us to discover a timeless witnessing technique.

> Philip, like Andrew and Peter, was from the town of Bethsaida. Philip found Nathanael and told him, "We have found the one Moses wrote about in the Law, and about whom the prophets also wrote—Jesus of Nazareth, the son of Joseph."
>
> "Nazareth! Can anything good come from there?" Nathanael asked. "Come and see," said Philip. (John 1:44–46)

Do you see it? It's right there! It's a three-step method (every good scriptural outline has to have three parts, or it just won't "preach!") that is just as effective today as it was when Jesus was calling his first disciples to himself.

Step 1. Find! "Philip found Nathanael . . . "

Step 2. Tell! " . . . and told him, 'We have found the one Moses wrote about in the Law, and about whom the prophets also wrote, Jesus of Nazareth, the son of Joseph.' "

Step 3. Invite! "'Come and see,' said Philip."

How to Find Your Target Focus

Oh, so you think that talking about a "target focus" makes witnessing sound clinical and non-relational? Not so! Having a carefully selected target (the person you are wanting to reach with the message of Jesus Christ) brings intentionality to your task and enables you to be a purpose-driven witness. In other words, it makes for much more effective witnesses.

At Mount Olive Lutheran Church we know exactly whom we are targeting in our ministry. We are trying to reach "Silicon Steve." (No, he is not a product of plastic surgery enhancement.) He is a 30-something married man who works long hours in the white-collar world of the high-tech computer industry. His household earns $65–75,000 each year, includes his wife and two children, makes frequent use of the recreational opportunities of Northern California, and is de-churched. (He was involved previously in church during his growing up years, but fell away during college.) "For the sake of the children" Silicon Steve is looking for a church that is relevant to life in the 1990s.

When we developed a profile of our community (a demographic study), we identified common threads among its residents that gave birth to Steve's profile. While we target Steve in our ministry, we are thrilled, of course, to receive whomever the Lord brings to us. However, sharpening our focus allows us to take careful aim with the Word and our resources of time and money. It is the difference between shooting with a high-powered rifle equipped with a scope and firing a sawed-off shotgun. Both guns will hit a target, but the rifle enables you to be a better steward of your ammunition. The rifle is also a lot less messy!

I think Jesus had this in mind when he told the parable of the sower and the seed (Mark 4:1–20). Certainly, the seed, or the Word of God, is to be sown everywhere; but when it is planted in good, fertile soil, it will most easily take root, producing saving faith. Establishing a target helps us from the very beginning to find the most receptive soil.

Once we are able to identify the kind of people who make up our community, we know who it is the Lord has called us to reach. Our ministry, while never changing the substance of what we believe, offers a style that intentionally and effectively addresses the needs of our community's Silicon Steves as we seek to lead them into a life-changing encounter with Jesus Christ.

Whether we are attempting to reach a whole community or one person at a time, establishing our target focus is critical. The disciples had no difficulty establishing their target focus. They found, told, and invited people who knew and trusted them. They started with their personal relationships. That's where we need to begin, too.

Make a list of your friends, family, work associates, classmates, teammates, etc., who do not know the Lord. On the last page of this book you will find a copy of the form that I use in developing my game plan to reach unbelievers. Copy this form in quantity and each month fill one in for each person on your list whom you consider your target focus. Don't take on every name on your list as you begin. Be selective. Ask yourself, "Who am I most equipped to reach? Which friendships are my strongest trust relationships?" Acknowledging your limitations narrows your focus and makes you a more effective witness. You cannot bring the saving Word of God to the whole world, not even to all of your acquaintances at one time.

Prayer: Enlisting the Front Office

"Then Jesus told his disciples a parable to show them that they should always pray and not give up" (Luke 18:1).

"Until now you have not asked for anything in my name. Ask and you will receive, and your joy will be complete" (John 16:24).

"Therefore I tell you, whatever you ask for in prayer, believe that you have received it, and it will be yours" (Mark 11:24).

"The prayer of a righteous man is powerful and effective" (James 5:16b).

"My prayer is not for them alone. I pray also for those who will believe in me through their message" (John 17:20).

Do you get the idea that Christians are to include prayer in their witnessing efforts? I am convinced that unless prayer is an integral part of our witnessing game plan, we will never accomplish the task the Lord calls us to. If ever there was a prayer concern within the will of God, one for which we can count on the Lord's affirmation, it is the salvation of an individual who has resisted God's call to new life.

Previously, we considered how the "Front Office" (God) is at work preparing individuals to hear and respond to the Gospel. Our prayers are a powerful catalyst in seeing that happen. You've read the verses: " . . . prayers of a righteous man are powerful and effective." "Ask and you will receive, and your joy will be made complete." We even read of Jesus praying for "those who will believe in me through their message."

Now, ask yourself the hard question: Are you praying for those you have listed on your game plan form the way you should? I'm not talking about the casual, once in a while kind of prayer that tags along like a p.s. at the end of a letter. "Oh, yeah . . . God, will you, ah, help Jackie to know you, too." I am referring to committed, faithful prayer on behalf of someone you care about. Do you "always pray and not give up hope"?

When we become involved in the circumstances that surround a person's place in eternity, we are entering a spiritual war zone. Apart from the Lord, people are in Satan's territory, and the Enemy doesn't want to give them up. Prayer becomes a powerful weapon in the church's warfare for the lost. We can be victorious in this battle because Jesus won the war. He fought and defeated sin, death, and the power of the devil, and his victory is for all people, including those who have yet to believe.

Prayer becomes an integral part of our witnessing game plan when we commit to pray daily for each person we have named on a Witnessing Game Plan sheet. Notice the check-off boxes on the game plan for every day of the month. A visible reminder, like a prayer check, is a valuable tool for intentional and powerful prayer.

As I become friendly with those I have placed on my game plan sheets, I let them know that I intend to pray for them. Once they recover from the shock of the news, I ask if they have any needs that I can pray about. (Most people forget very quickly that I am a "professional pray-er.") The first few times that I ask, I usually receive a "Well I can't think of anything right now" kind of answer. That's okay. I just keep on asking. As these relationships develop, at times they actually ask me to pray for their needs; that is a real joy! I make individual prayer needs my concern by writing them on the back of the game plan sheet and including them in my prayers every day. I use the check-off boxes on the game plan sheets as a reminder to pray specifically for opportunities to *tell* each person my story about Jesus and to *invite* them to worship, fellowship activities and even a barbecue in my backyard with other friends from church.

I also ask the Lord to show me ways to let them know that I care about them. Following my prayer time, I will frequently make contact by writing notes, sending a card, making a phone call, or by stopping by for a visit. These efforts grow out of the time I spend before the Lord, and he greatly blesses them, expanding my relationships with the people I want to witness to and creating new Cross Points, enabling me to share the story of Jesus in me.

Keeping Track of Cross Points

I am grateful that the Lord has given me a wife who knows my weaknesses and does a great job compensating for them. I have a terrible memory! As Kathy stands with me at the church door each Sunday morning, greeting the people of Mount Olive, she will regularly whisper names of new people that she knows I don't remember. The rest of the week, I cruise through each day with my trusty binder-sized Day-Timer open, feverishly scribbling notes. If I lost my Bible, I could handle that, I'd buy another one. Kathy is convinced that if I lost my Day-Timer, I'd have to retire.

One of the most important ways in which I can communicate my caring for someone else is to listen to what they have to say and then remember it. That, as you now know, is not easy for me to do. When it comes to remembering the details that make witnessing personal, I'll take all the help I can get.

It is especially important to remember Cross Points. They are the "stuff" (that's a Silicon Valley word for something that is very important but doesn't have a real name) of witnessing. They open up opportunities for conversation and provide the contemporary context for my story so that it connects with someone else's life.

I keep track of Cross Points by writing them down as part of my game plan sheets. When a friend whom I have targeted to reach for Jesus Christ tells me that she is worried because her mother is very ill and might die, I want to remember that. I will, of course, add that concern to the prayer list I maintain for her needs, but I will also record it in the Cross Points section of her game plan sheet. Once I have done that, I will write down a corresponding experience in my own life that might bring a word of encouragement and an opportunity to talk about how the Lord helped me through a similarly difficult time. Each day as I pray for her, I am also able to review all of the various Cross Points that I am hoping to use as tools to tell her about Christ. It is exciting to hear someone say, "Oh, you remembered that my mom is sick and you're praying for her? Wow, that's great. Thanks!"

Let's face it, no matter how well-intentioned we are, remembering everything that would be helpful for witnessing is impossible. Write it down; God gave us an alphabet for a reason!

Telling and Inviting

Kathy and I have had a regular weekly date night for the last eight years. We do lots of things together, usually spending more money on babysitting than on ourselves. We may go out to dinner (hamburger, fries, soda, and the romantic lighting of the golden arches), visit friends (we are really good at inviting ourselves for dinner), go shopping (a very dangerous date), attend music theater (we've had tickets for several years), or take in a movie.

We rate movie theaters by price (we refuse to pay the big bucks) and how badly our shoes stick to the floor under our seats (the cheaper the show, the stickier the floor). For Christmas each year we usually receive gifts of movie tickets from church members who encourage our date night. That's when we go all out; we attend a full-priced evening show, buy refreshments (rather than stopping at the grocery store on the way) and even wear our good shoes.

We arrive early to get the full effect, have competitions answering the trivia questions flashed on the screen prior to the film, and watch the previews with the interest of a Siskel and Ebert. Then it happens: *Feature Presentation* flashes across the screen. I put my arm around Kathy's shoulders (knowing that it will probably take a paramedic to restore circulation when the movie is over), and we settle in for an hour and a half of the real stuff, the centerpiece of our evening. The story is about to begin.

Telling and inviting form the centerpiece of the witnessing experience once we have found our target focus. Not that everything else that happens before the telling and inviting isn't important. We've already established that it is. But telling and inviting is the time when we share our faith story; Jesus becomes the focus, the Holy Spirit goes to work in a powerful way, and the invitation is offered.

Because most people will hear about Jesus and will come to trust him as their Savior as a result of a personal relationship, it makes sense for us to intentionally foster and develop these special relationships. One of the best ways to do that is through conversations in casual, informal gatherings.

Guess Who Is Coming to Dinner

Have you ever noticed in the Scriptures how often Jesus did his telling and inviting during a meal? Take a look sometime. It's amazing and definitely not coincidental. Eating together makes the walls that separate us disappear. (There is just something about slurping soup together or dripping gravy on your dress that makes everyone equal!) It creates a casual, non-threatening environment where distractions are at a minimum and conversation can flow. Consider the familiar example of Zacchaeus in Luke 19.

Zacchaeus wasn't very well liked. He was one of THEM, a tax collector, someone who had sold himself to the Romans so he could live "high on the hog" off everyone else's misfortune. At least that's how the town folk pegged him. Since he wasn't very tall, he also made a wonderful target for the latest "short jokes." (Remember, those were the days, before civil rights, when harassment was the rule, not the exception.)

It is said that everyone loves a parade, and apparently this little tax collector wasn't any different. Jesus was going to pass through Jericho, Zacchaeus' home town, but such a sizable crowd had gathered and so totally had they lined the narrow streets that Zacchaeus couldn't see. He had heard about Jesus, and he wanted at least a glimpse of him, but all he could see were the backs of heads and shoulders. He was used to circumstances like this, always being on the short end of the stick (sorry!), watching for better vantage points. A sycamore tree provided a nice one.

"Zacchaeus, come down immediately. I must stay at your house today" (v. 5).

Jesus had his attention. He knew Jesus' name, but how did Jesus know his? "Sure, Jesus, come on. I'd be happy to have you over to my house." ("That'll teach everyone to make fun of me. Jesus didn't ask to go to any of their homes. No . . . , he asked to come to mine!")

Now look closely at Luke 19. Something happened between verses 7 and 8. My guess is, dinner! Notice what it says at the beginning of verse 8, "But Zacchaeus stood up . . ." I believe that he and Jesus, plus a good sized group of followers (a big dinner wasn't a problem for a high roller like Zacchaeus) had been reclining at a table, enjoying a nice dinner. During this time Jesus did what he always did, he spoke of the kingdom of

God, the Gospel, and he invited Zacchaeus to a new and changed life.

Jesus didn't "tell" and "invite" Zacchaeus as part of a big street rally in Jericho. He did it in a casual, relational manner over dinner. And it worked, too! "Today salvation has come to this house," Jesus announced, "because this man, too, is a son of Abraham. For the Son of Man came to seek and to save what was lost" (Luke 19:9–10).

Jesus did the same when, over a meal of five loaves and two fish, he fed and taught the 5,000 (Luke 9:10–17). He revealed himself as the resurrected Christ during dinner with two disciples in the village of Emmaus (Luke 24:13–35). He reinstated Peter, who had denied him three times on the night of his arrest and trial, after a breakfast of grilled fish (John 21:1–19). And Jesus reveals himself to us today each time we receive the marvelous blessings of the Communion meal that he has prepared for us. A coincidence? I don't think so!

I use the section of the game plan sheets labeled "Opportunites for Telling and Inviting" to strategically plan and list times when I can be in a casual environment with the person on whom I am focusing. It can be over a meal, on the golf course, sitting and soaking in our spa, anywhere and anytime where an opportunity to tell my story could arise.

There are also countless ways to tell and invite, apart from arranged occasions. Impromptu talks around the coffeepot and even an unplanned meeting at the gutter while setting out the garbage cans have provided potential for the crucified and risen Savior to reveal himself. If we will learn to live life with our witnessing eyes open and if we will cultivate informal relationships with the people we have listed on our game plan sheets, we will be amazed at the opportunities.

Celebrate the Little Things

I like to keep track of the witnessing successes that occur as the game plan develops. It's really easy to track the conversions that occur, but those are seldom as frequent as I'd like. That makes it all the more important for me to record and celebrate all of the little victories, like inviting my friends to worship with me on Christmas Eve and having them actually show up, having the checkout clerk remember the dot on my watch and ask if I had my "quiet time with the Lord today," enjoying a great time of relationship-building conversation over a simple and relaxing meal. When I am alert, I quickly discover that the reasons to celebrate are endless.

We often set goals for ourselves that are so difficult to achieve that we get discouraged along the way. Learning, instead, to give thanks and praise to God for little blessings will help us stick with our Witnessing Game Plan while we diligently and intentionally look for opportunities for the Gospel and the Holy Spirit to go to work.

It's time to give it a try! You've got a focus, a message, a story, and a game plan. Let's get out of the bleachers and onto the field!

Onto the Field

The Witnessing Game Plan sheet provides a very practical tool to assist your witnessing. Make several photocopies of the blank form on the last page of this book. As you think and pray about the various relationships that you have targeted, begin to fill in the blanks. Gradually the blanks will be completed as you continue to grow in relationship with your target focus. Refer to the game plan sheet daily for prayer and as a reminder of the manner in which God has prepared you to witness.

Chapter 9

What Do I Do if It Works?

"Time out, Ump, time out!" The coach ran over to home plate to counsel with a very bewildered four-year old. "What's the matter?"

"What do I do if I hit the ball, Coach?"(It was obvious that this T-ball rookie never expected the ball to move off the tee.)

"Run," the coach answered, "just run as fast as you can." (I knew the coach was in trouble; he never told the batter which direction to run if he hit the ball.)

The opposing team got set again. They were so cute! Little brightly colored shirts dotted the field. Baseball caps, adjusted to the smallest possible size, balanced precariously atop little ears, obscuring facial features—at least they kept the sun from burning their noses! Oversized gloves hung down from their arms, making it appear that a team of mutant lobsters had taken over the field.

The bat moved back and forth, measuring for the perfect swing. Hesitancy was written all over the batter's face.

"You got'ta swing now, you got'ta swing!"

Those words of exasperated encouragement came from the end of the dugout where the coaches sat. These were a special breed of men!

The bat started to move forward. You could tell that this wasn't a warm-up swing. This was the real thing. He was going to hit the ball—or at least knock the tee over. The trained T-ball afficionado (that's a "T-ball parent" for the uninitiated) could see that the batter was going to hit the ball because his eyes were closed. (They all close their eyes when they swing. I think you have to be able to do that before they let you play!)

The ball leaped off the tee and started its way down the third base line. He had hit the ball, and it was staying fair!

"Now, run! Run!"

He took off at incredible speed, down the third base line and out into left field, passing his teammate who was running from third to home.

The defense wasn't a bit confused. When the ball stopped rolling and the players had finished arguing over who would get to pick it up, the victor started to chase the hitter. It was a sight to behold. Never has an Olympic ice skater formed more perfect figure 8's. They covered the entire outfield with coaches from both teams running behind, trying to stop play in order to instruct their players properly about what they were supposed to do when they hit the ball.

Knowing "what to do" when an opportunity presents itself is really a matter of expectation and anticipation, of learning to plan ahead. We are told to think before we speak; to drive defensively, always being aware and always planning routes of escape in case of trouble. We assume our financial portfolios deserve careful planning, because we are anxious to get the most out of every dollar invested. Hours of tedious work go into the design and construction of new buildings. (There are more examples than I've got space.)

Why invest so much effort? Why are people able to be proactive rather than reactive? Because they expect results!

How about it? Do you expect to see results from your witnessing efforts? Do you expect people actually to come to faith when you share your story with them? What are you going to do if it works? Do you have a plan that will go into effect when she says to you, "You know, I believe this stuff. What do I do next?"

Announcing, "I don't know, I've never gotten this far before," or "I haven't a clue, let's go see the pastor," is like running figure 8's in the outfield. It just isn't going to cut it. When God uses your witness as the Holy Spirit's tool to spark faith in the life of someone you know, the responsibility to walk with them through the entire experience belongs to no one but you.

So, what are you going to do if it works?

"Jesus Didn't Tell Us about This!"

The disciples were afraid, confused, and disappointed. It hadn't happened at all the way they thought it would. They had expected Israel to become a glorious kingdom once again, restored to her golden days as in the time of David and Solomon. The Roman army would be defeated, they believed. Jesus would be on the throne of Israel, and they, the disciples, would help him rule. That's what they had expected. Instead, they were hiding out in a locked room.

The last couple of months had been a real roller-coaster ride. Their emotions were all over the place! They had seen Jesus crucified, resurrected, and ascended. It is safe to assume that everywhere they went people were laughing at them, "Where's Jesus, now? Things sure didn't pan out the way you thought they would!" The Romans and the Jewish leaders who had crucified Jesus just a few weeks before hadn't disappeared either. Maybe lying low for a while wasn't such a bad idea after all.

It wasn't the Lord's idea, however. Ten days earlier, on the day of his ascension into heaven, Jesus had promised that something important was about to happen. "You will receive power when the Holy Spirit comes on you; and you will be my witnesses in Jerusalem, and in all Judea and Samaria, and to the ends of the earth" (Acts 1:8). So, since they were not supposed to leave Jerusalem until the Spirit came, they waited. For 10 days they waited, until that fateful Sunday right around 9 a.m.

What sounded like a rushing wind on a calm day, what passed for tongues of fire, the outpouring of the Holy Spirit, followed by people speaking in unknown languages, would have a way of grabbing anyone's attention. The disciples were no exception. On the Day of Pentecost, for the first time, Jesus' closest followers were able to tell their story of their Master in a manner in which all the pieces made sense. Peter spoke on behalf of them all.

God had gathered quite an intimidating crowd for Peter's first sermon. It turned out to be a cross-cultural congregation for which God provided the disciples as interpreters. People from all over the known world had crowded into Jerusalem to worship. Thousands of listeners pressed around those 12 apostles (one of them brand new) plus a substantial group of 108 miscellaneous followers of the crucified, risen, and ascended Christ (Acts 1:15). Regardless of the demographic makeup of the group, I don't think it would have been my dream congregation for the first time I stepped into the pulpit! But what a sermon it was! Three thousand people came to faith and were baptized that morning!

"When the people heard this, they were cut to the heart and said to Peter and the other apostles, 'Brothers, what shall we do?' " (Acts 2:37).

For the first time ever the disciples told their story about Jesus, and it worked! What to do now? They didn't have the privilege of referring the people to someone else. Their expert had just ascended into heaven. They were on the spot, and they had to give the answer.

Peter replied [for all of them], "Repent and be baptized, every one of you, in the name of Jesus Christ for the forgiveness of your sins. And you will receive the gift of the Holy Spirit. The promise is for you and your children and for all who are far off— for all whom the Lord our God will call." With many other words he warned them; and he pleaded with them, "Save yourselves from this corrupt generation." (Acts 2:38–40)

Peter expected change to occur in the lives of people who heard the Gospel, and he was ready and able to offer a "next step." His response to their question included two key ingredients that are important for us in our witnessing. He invited people to action, and he provided affirmation, never once getting in the way of his hearers' Spirit-led response to the call of God on their lives. His guidance allowed them to be affirmed in the faith that the Holy Spirit was creating in them. It allowed them to drink freely from the life-giving water that Jesus offers!

You've Got to Let Them Drink

In the Kalahari Desert of southern Africa, it usually rains during March and April. In 1979 it never rained. The grasses that provide fodder for countless species of animal life changed from green to tan to lifeless straw.

For the wildebeest it was time to move. Many generations of wildebeest had made the trek north to the only place where water would be found in a time of drought, Lake Xau and Lake Ngami. Numbering more than 90,000, the animals spent little time feeding. Without moisture they were incapable of digesting what they ate. They needed to get to the water and to better food as soon as possible. They were able to travel about 25 miles each night, walking north in the cooler evening hours so as to avoid the horrible heat and dehydration.

One night as they continued their journey for survival, this massive herd of wildebeest suddenly stopped. Confused, they milled around in uncertainty. Stretched across their path was a wire fence. The Kuki foot and mouth disease control fence had been erected to separate the domestic livestock from the wild herds that were feared to be carriers of the disease. While it kept the domestic and wild herds from mixing, it also kept the wildebeest and other animals from the life-giving water that they needed during the drought.

They were frustrated. Their instincts told them that they had to head north where the water would be found. But now the only way for them to continue was to turn east along the fence, making their journey 100 miles longer and, eventually, bringing them to the reality of yet another fence. They could smell the water, it was only 25 miles away. But in the chaos, the heat, and the dust one after another collapsed. Scavengers began their awful work even before death had occurred. The wildebeest knew the water was there, but people had put obstacles in their path that they found impossible to overcome.

We could be guilty of doing the same thing to those with whom we witness! If we share our faith story, include the fundamentals of the Gospel, get people excited about what life can be like with Jesus, and then leave them high and dry because we don't know what to do next, in reality we would be letting them pile up against a "fence" of our own making. They would miss the fullness of new life that Jesus offers. What a horrible failure on our part! When the Holy Spirit calls people to the living water of Jesus, they will respond. It is our responsibility to show them how to drink.

Inviting and Affirming

There is no question that Peter was "flying by the seat of his pants" on the Day of Pentecost. He didn't have time to prepare. He hadn't spent the previous week doing the proper exegetical, hermenuetical, and homiletical preparation (that's pastor talk for "sermon study") in order to present a carefully outlined message. He didn't need to. God wired him directly into the Holy Spirit; he got his words right from the source. And that's reason enough for us to pay attention to what he said.

"Repent and be baptized" (Acts 2:38). God's words through Peter led 3,000 people in that mob to drink the living water of salvation in Jesus.

Peter's words are a call to action, and yet, at the same time, they are also the fulfillment of a work already initiated by the Holy Spirit. When I have the opportunity to be a companion in people's discovery of salvation, and when I believe that God has their attention, it is exciting for me to ask for their response. I will usually ask something very theological-sounding like, "What do you think about all this stuff we've talked about? Do you believe it, too?" They may respond, "Yes, it's great!" or "Wow! I never knew that God had so much to offer for my life!" Responses are as varied as personalities. However they word it, their response will prompt me then to ask the big question (this is when the "fences" are knocked down, and they discover that the living water is for them, too). "Are you saying that you also believe in Jesus and confess him as your Lord and Savior?"

I use the words, "believe in and confess" instead of "asking Jesus into your heart," because the Scriptures give reason to ask the question this way. The concluding part of 1 Cor. 12:3 tells why. "No one can say, 'Jesus is Lord,' except by the Holy Spirit."

Because my friend has said, "Yes, I believe and I want to confess Jesus as my Savior," there is no reason for him to "ask Jesus" into his heart. Jesus is already there! (Remember, "No one can say, 'Jesus is Lord,' except by the Holy Spirit.") God has knocked down the fence and done the work of salvation. Salvation is not something we decide to do, it is God's work. And, believing and trusting God for salvation is also his work. The Holy Spirit enables us to respond and believe.

When I teach this critical concept to my Christianity 101 classes (our Adult Information Class at Mount Olive) we pretend that we are making a visit to the morgue. (Hang in there, I know it's strange.) I have one of the men lie down on a table as if he were dead, while we talk about what it means to be spiritually dead and unable to save ourselves. I then hold over him "life" (usually my half-full coffee cup) and say, "Jim, I know you are dead, but 'here' is life. All you have to do to come back to life is to reach up and take it for yourself." Then I ask the class, "Can he do that?"

"No!", they respond in unison. (They are so well trained!)

"Why not?"

"Because he's dead. Dead people can't do anything for themselves."

"Right!"

When we are spiritually dead due to the sinfulness that separates us from God, we are incapable of making ourselves believers. I cannot decide to believe. Not only can God alone offer new life, but he is also the only one who can enable me to believe and thereby receive new life.

Peter's call to action in Acts 2:38 ("Repent and be baptized") not only invites people to experience God's living water, but it also offers great words of affirmation that say it is okay to drink. After the Gospel message is shared, words of affirmation summarize its sweet message, assuring people it is really for them. "Go ahead, rejoice in it!"

That kind of encouragement needs to be offered not only once, but repeatedly, just as repetition is important in all of our learning processes. I remember my high school speech and debate coach's often repeated advice, "Tell them what you are going to say, say it, and then tell them what you just said." Peter does exactly that. There is nothing substantive in verses 38–40 that Peter hadn't said earlier. He repeats this affirmation because the message of a Savior who died and rose again is radically new all by itself. For people hearing this for the first time it's difficult to accept that the God of all creation loves them and desires a personal relationship with them. Repetition helps us to say, "I'm excited for you! Experience what your Savior has to offer. Take a drink. Know his love and salvation. Begin to understand and receive the inheritance that he offers."

What Do I Do if I Swing and Miss?

"What happens if it doesn't work? What if she says no when I ask if she also believes in Jesus and confesses him as her Lord and Savior?"

The reality of witnessing is that not everyone will believe. Many will resist the glorious blessings the Lord offers to them. Some will never believe, while others only need more time. When a no comes, don't let it defeat you! If you have intentionally built a caring relationship, there will be other opportunities to ask again.

God gives us a wonderful promise in Is. 55:11, "So is my word that goes out from my mouth: It will not return to me empty, but will accomplish what I desire and achieve the purpose for which I sent it." You see, even if your friend said no, God's Word, nevertheless, was doing some important work. Whenever the Gospel is shared, the Holy Spirit is present, doing the necessary work to create faith. Sometimes it takes longer to remove the defenses of unbelief and bring down the walls of resistance. Other times, the individual just needs to learn more. That's why it is so important that we do not give up. The person to whom you are witnessing may need to hear your story of Jesus many times before it sinks in and God can convert her. Each time that you are able to share or to ask if she believes, you are creating a Cross Point for future opportunities.

I enjoy gardening. No matter where Kathy and I have lived, there has always been space for a vegetable garden, even if it amounts to no more than a tomato plant or two. During the year of my ministerial internship we had a huge garden because an elderly woman next door offered us the use of her backyard. We planted every vegetable that would grow in northern New Jersey. The rows were perfectly furrowed, the plants staked appropriately. We saw to it that the garden did not lack for fertilizer or water. What it did lack was the constant warmth of the sun. (The growing season in New Jersey differs from our native California. Because the New Jersey winters are longer, the harvest is later. Now that may seem rather obvious to you, but we missed it completely.

All spring and summer we worked, weeded, fertilized, watered, and cultivated. The plants grew nicely but the harvest was slow in coming. When the middle of August arrived, so did the time for us to return to the seminary in St. Louis for my final year of school. It was difficult to say good-bye to all of our friends. It was equally difficult to walk away from the garden that was only a week or two from being harvested. The harvest was definitely going to occur, and it was going to happen without us. Even though Kathy and I did the work, we were not going to be the people who would enjoy its bounty. After we had returned to St. Louis we received reports that our efforts continued to bring forth fruit until early that fall.

The Lord will provide you with many opportunites to witness. Some will involve a lot of work as the Lord uses you to carefully plant the message of Jesus through caring conversations and cultivated relationships. In other cases God will bless your efforts to lead a friend into a saving relationship with Jesus after only a brief time of witnessing. God is the Lord of the harvest, and he has declared that the harvest is ready. What he now needs are all kinds of people, like you and me, to do their part: planting, fertilizing, cultivating, and harvesting. As we go about our work he makes us into a great team of witnesses who strive together to accomplish a wonderful task.

Onto the Field

Peter's message on the day of Pentecost (Acts 2:14–41) shows that witnessing is both invitational and affirming. Think through the manner in which you would offer both invitation and affirmation in the following scenario:

For the last few months you have been building a relationship with your friend, Steve. He has been to your home for dinner, played with you on the church softball team, and even attended Christmas worship with you. Each time you have witnessed to him, the conversation provided new opportunities for the Gospel, and yet he has not believed. Today is different. Steve has just finished saying, "I understand what you mean. I believe what you've said to me about Jesus. Does that mean I'm a Christian?"

It's your turn. What will you say to Steve that is both invitational and affirming?

Chapter 10

The Care and Feeding of Rookies

From where I was sitting, I could see only white robes, red stoles, and waistlines, some of them more substantial than others (the red stoles, of course). In turn, each person so dressed placed his hand on my head, spoke a portion of Scripture, and gave me a blessing. We stood up, we sat down (in our church we do that a lot), we prayed, we spoke and sang, and then it was done. I was a newly ordained and installed pastor!

Now what in the world was I going to do?

I was graduated, accredited, ordained, installed, and scared to death! I was part of the team, but I didn't really know my position, even though I looked like I fit the role. I could wear the team uniform (a white robe) with the best of them. My new silk stoles looked pretty cool, too. I lined my office shelves with imposing-looking books (many of which I still haven't read) and hung tastefully framed diplomas on the wall behind my desk. (To this day, I'm still not sure what the one in Latin says!) I had watched pastors do their thing for years. The difference was that this congregation was now my congregation, and I wasn't sure what "my thing" was at all. They were real people with very real needs, one of which was to have a real pastor. What they were getting was a very green rookie!

At least I was only the assistant pastor; the senior pastor would be around to help me answer all the burning questions, such as, what do pastors really do between Sunday mornings? However, three weeks after I arrived, he left for a 10-week study leave in Germany! He didn't take off for school just to be mean or to find out if I was going to sink or swim; it had all been planned long before I got there. The truth of the matter was that God was about the task of writing my story, and, as it turned out, those 10 weeks formed a very important chapter.

Most stories have a hero, and mine was no exception. His name was Bill Duerr, Sr., pastor extraordinaire, with 56 years of ministry wisdom. At Redeemer Church, Huntington Beach, Calif., Pastor Bill worked part-time as visitation pastor and full-time as my example. During those 10 weeks he helped me to become part of the congregation, to become assimilated, and to understand my role as one of the pastors. I would have been lost without him. All rookie pastors should be so blessed by God!

Confusion and fear are normal experiences for rookies of all kinds, from professional athletes to pastors, at least for those who are honest about their feelings. Individuals who have just experienced God's saving work in Jesus Christ also experience confusion and anxiety. In every case, rookies need someone who will take them under their wing and provide the care that assimilates them and makes them truly part of the team.

When the Lord uses us to communicate the Gospel in such a way that someone comes to faith in Jesus, it stands to reason our warm wing and watchful eye will best serve that new Christian. We have an obligation to that person. Ready or not, we have become another human being's spiritual example, mentor, expert, coach, and parent. It is now our responsibility to help this baby believer discover what it means to be a Christian and how to become an assimilated, active part of a congregation of other believers. These spiritual babies, through their adoption into the family of God, are now part of our family. When we neglect our responsibility, it is as if we have made this newly believing person a spiritual orphan. The news media regularly reports stories of abandoned children and their parents who are arrested for the horrible crime. I wish that Christians would be more horrified by the awful "child abuse" we unintentionally perpetrate when new believers are ignored.

"Follow Your Shot"

I had a basketball coach who drove me crazy repeating one phrase over and over again, "Follow your shot, Gibson!" Now, I have to acknowledge that I have a very pretty jump shot. I used to practice my form all the time. I looked good! I didn't make many baskets, but I was sharp to look at. That's why the coach would scream for me to follow my shot, to run toward the basket as soon as I had shot the ball in an attempt to retrieve the inevitable rebound and possibly try again. It is a fundamental principle of basketball. (That's probably why my basketball career was so short-lived.)

I'd like to coach a few Gospel witnesses and drive them crazy by yelling, "Follow your shot!" We can expect a lot of missed shots and rebounds when sharing our faith. That doesn't mean that we've done a poor job; it's just the reality of witnessing in an unbelieving world. But when we score, our follow-through is to assure that our new "little brother or sister in Christ" will become firmly grounded in an ongoing relationship with the living God. Tossing the Gospel message to someone and then running to the next "shooting" opportunity is a very poor way for family members to treat one another. Follow-up is critical.

Paul and Barnabas understood this principle; they would have made great basketball players! Check out Acts 15:36: "Some time later Paul said to Barnabas, 'Let us go back and visit the brothers in all the towns where we preached the word of the Lord and see how they are doing.' "

While Paul and Barnabas' personalities clashed, splitting their powerful evangelistic team (Acts 15:37–41), they had no disagreement about the fact that the people they had led to the Lord needed them. New believers have much to learn.

There is another occasion recorded in the book of Acts where follow-up is shown very clearly. Paul spent a great deal of time with a couple named Priscilla and Aquila, even for a while living and making tents with them (Acts 18:1–3). After Paul left them in order to resume his missionary journey, Priscilla and Aquila made sure that new believers continued to grow and were equipped to do the work of witnessing themselves.

One such young believer was a Jew named Apollos, a native of Alexandria, who came to Ephesus. A learned man with a thorough knowledge of the Scriptures, he had been instructed in the way of the Lord, and he spoke with great fervor and taught accurately about Jesus, though he knew only the baptism of John. Shortly after arriving he began to speak boldly in the Ephesian synagogue. When Priscilla and Aquila heard him, they invited him to their home and explained to him the way of God more adequately. When Apollos wanted to go to Achaia, the brothers encouraged him and wrote to the disciples there to welcome him. On arriving, he was a great help to those who by grace had believed, for he vigorously refuted the Jews in public debate, proving from the Scriptures that Jesus was the Christ (Acts 18:24–28). Follow-through works! Apollos' story proves that.

Making disciples is more than initially telling people about Jesus; it includes teaching them about their faith and equipping them to tell their story to others, so that they too can get out of the bleachers and onto the field.

Okay, Coach
Here's What You Need to Do!

Help Her Find the Right Team

You've been praying for her, building a relationship with her, identifying Cross Points, and sharing your story. God has done his awesome work of enabling her to believe and confess Jesus as her Savior, and now she needs a place where she can grow and understand her new faith. She needs to become part of a caring team that will encourage her. She needs to become part of a congregation!

Hopefully it will be your church. It's the easiest place for you to help her become assimilated. It's the church you know best. Your friends in the church can most easily become her friends. Your enthusiasm about your congregation and its ministry will be contagious.

But church is more than just a place for her to belong, to build friendships and to put down spiritual roots. It is also a place of worship, growth, and service. As you walk with her through this process of assimilation she will learn through your example why it is important that she grow in faith and come together regularly with other believers to celebrate her new life in

Christ. Don't take anything for granted; a new Christian may not understand many things that are second nature to you. You may need to spend time explaining what is happening in the worship service and why. Lots of first-timers at worship appreciate a walk through the bulletin and the building. Help them learn the ropes, so they won't look as green as they feel. (You'll probably have to ask your pastor a few questions and learn something yourself in the process.)

As you guide her through the steps of discovering the right team (church), be aware that your church may not be the place for her! (Oh-oh! Did I really say that?) Congregations are like people; they have personalities. We get along fine with some personalities and not so well with others. The same is true with churches. In the case of your new sister in Christ, the first concern has to be for her relationship with the Lord, not the numerical growth of your congregation (while that would certainly be nice).

Here's what I would do. I would talk with her about the importance of having a home congregation where she can worship and grow in her faith, and I would definitely invite her to my church. After all, I go there because it is the best around! I'd tell her about our various ministries, our pastor and staff, and the great people there. But I would also promise that, after a while, if she didn't like it, I would go with her to other churches until she found one that fit her personality, gifts, and needs. By telling her that, I am communicating my love and concern for her and letting her know that we regard her as a valuable person, not just another statistic. Chances are, your church will be the perfect place for her; after all, you are there!

Finalize the Adoption

When you have had the privilege of leading a person to first-time faith in the Lord, you may also get the privilege of bringing that person to the next step, Baptism. Since pastors ultimately are involved with Baptism, don't hesitate to involve your own pastor early on as you discuss this with your new Christian siblings. Your pastor can assist you in explaining why Baptism is important and what it means. Make sure you are with your new Christian sibling for the first meeting with your pastor, whether you are discussing Baptism or something else. While you know that pastors don't bite, your friend may not be so sure!

Frequently, the people with whom you share your faith will have been baptized already, but they haven't been in church for quite a while. Their Baptisms are still valid today. Even though they may need a lot of orientation and instruction, they don't need to undergo a second Baptism as long as they were baptized in the name of the Triune God. (Remember, a lot of false churches and cults practice baptisms that are not acceptable to God. Someone with that kind of background will need to be baptized.) Since God never goes back on his promises, and he is the one doing the work in Baptism, there is no baptismal statute of limitations! The apostle Paul writes in Eph. 4:4–6 about the effectiveness of one Baptism: "There is one body and one Spirit—just as you were called to one hope when you were called—one Lord, one faith, one baptism; one God and Father of all, who is over all and through all and in all."

Speaking of Baptism, don't forget the kids! If your new believing friend is a parent, make sure you ask if he has any children and whether or not they are baptized. Not too long ago we baptized a Dad and three kids; it was a very exciting morning!

Teach the Fundamentals

At Mount Olive we call it "Christianity 101." Other congregations refer to it as the "pastor's class." Whatever you call it, use it! A Bible study class, taught by a pastor or another seasoned Christian, is a great way to help people new to the Lord get their spiritual feet wet. (It's a great refresher course for you, too.) Usually these classes cover the basics of the Christian faith in both doctrine and practice, provide information about the church's history, purpose, and method of ministry; provide biographies of the staff, and explain what it means to be a member of the congregation. This opportunity to spend some quality time with the pastor and to meet many other new people like themselves comes at just the right time.

If you invite your friend to participate, make every effort to attend with him. If you can, show that you are truly excited about his new walk with the Lord by being involved in the learning process. Let him know you would enjoy discussing class topics with him, and especially offer to try to answer the questions that inevitably are going to arise. It will definitely cost you some time, but the benefits to you and to the new Christian will be awesome.

Build Team Relationships

Next to being the agent through whom God communicates the blessings of salvation, there is no greater thing you can do for new believers than to get them grounded, firmly rooted, in a small group that will provide ongoing loving and caring relationships to nurture them in their first hesitating steps as infant believers.

Unlike the so-called pastor's classes, these small groups can take many forms. At Mount Olive we offer "H.O.M.E." groups ("Homes of Ministry and Encouragement") where people study the Bible together, share and pray. Social groups, special needs groups (such as divorce recovery, AA, and other 12-step programs), and sports teams also serve new Christians. The variety is limited only by imagination and personal needs. Small groups provide a place where new people are not lost in the big crowd of the celebrating congregation. Their small size makes a new believer feel wanted and welcome, and it allows them, if they choose, to contribute their time and service, making a difference from the very start of their relationship with a congregation.

Help Her Find Her Position on the Field

This final section brings us full circle. The Lord wants new believers to grow and be nurtured and become able to bring others to faith in him. The goal is for every new Christian to become active on the field of life where witnessing can best take place. Few things are more exciting! (Unfortunately, a lot of congregations depend on the maternity ward for the growth of the church.)

The individuals who are new to the Lord have the highest number of unchurched friends, people for whom Christ died and with whom we need to share our faith. Invite new believers to begin immediately to talk with their unchurched friends about what has just happened to them and about their exciting church. If you can, meet some of their friends and, with their help, begin to build relationships that will provide future opportunities to tell their story and yours. The initial Cross Point is built in; you have a mutual friend who has just met Jesus as Savior!

Helping your new Christian brothers and sisters begin to share their faith is the most effective way to keep them from climbing on the bleachers. Witnessing will keep them where the real action is: out on the field, for the rest of their lives.

Onto the Field

"Be Prepared!" While the Boy Scouts' motto says a a lot about the philosophy of scouting, it says a mouthful about witnessing. Effective assimilation requires preparation so that proper guidance can be given to the new believer. Discovering your congregation's assimilation process will equip you with the information necessary to move your new sister or brother in Christ from new convert to reproducing member.

1. What are the requirements for membership at your church? How does someone become a member?

2. What procedure does your pastor follow for Baptism? Is prebaptismal counseling part of the procedure?

3. When is the next adult information class? What materials are required? Does your pastor use a particular Bible translation in class? Consider presenting your friend with the gift of a new Bible. If your new believing friend is a parent, find out if child care is provided while he or she attends classes.

4. Identify the various small-group opportunities at your church. Which one(s) would best fit your new believing friend's interests and situation in life? If possible, provide several options. Their schedule of availability will help him or her to make the final decision.

5. Share this book with your new sister or brother in Christ. It is never too soon to begin to witness. Show him or her how to use the Witnessing Game Plan sheet and assist him or her in developing a plan to reach his or her friends and family members with the good news of Jesus.

A Concluding Thought

We made another trip into the inner sanctum of the judge's chamber a few months ago. This time, Timothy Allen was sentenced to life as a Gibson. He got a new name, a new heritage, a chapter in the family history all his own, and a guaranteed inheritance.

It wasn't anything new to Tim, however, since he had already received a new name, a promised inheritance, and a new family history when he made the trip to the waters of Baptism on the day of his first adoption finalization.

As you live your life from this day forward, take a long hard look around you. There are lots of people like our Timothy, waiting to be adopted into the family of God. Countless people, many of them your friends and family members, need someone, maybe you, to speak to them the words of the Gospel and bring them into the presence of God himself, where they will hear him declare, "Welcome to my family. Welcome to the team!"

Isn't it obvious, if you want God to use you to reach unbelievers who cross your path, that you will need to stay out of the bleachers and on the field?